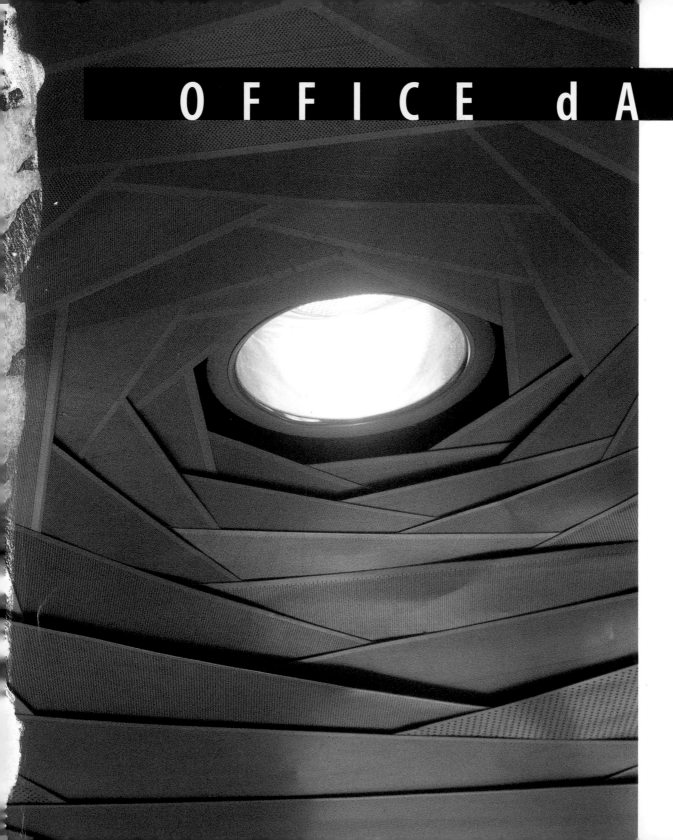

OFFICE dA

CONTEMPORARY
WORLD
ARCHITECTS

OFFICE dA

Works by
Mónica Ponce de León
and Nader Tehrani

Edited by
Rodolphe el-Khoury and
Oscar Riera Ojeda

Foreword by
Graham Owen

Photography by
Dan Bibb

Concept and Design by
Lucas H. Guerra
Oscar Riera Ojeda

ROCKPORT PUBLISHERS
GLOUCESTER, MASSACHUSETTS

First published in the United States of America by:
Rockport Publishers, Inc.
33 Commercial Street
Gloucester, Massachusetts 01930
Telephone: 978-282-9590
Fax: 978-283-2742
www.rockpub.com

Other distribution by Rockport Publishers, Inc.

ISBN 1-56496-546-5
10 9 8 7 6 5 4 3 2 1
Printed in China

Cover photograph: Fabrications: The Tectonic Garden, "Fabricating Coincidences" by Dan Bibb
Back cover photographs: (Top) Green House by Anton Grassl, (Bottom) Northeastern University Inter-Faith Spiritual Center by Dan Bibb
Back flap photograph: Mónica Ponce de León and Nader Tehrani by Richard Lee
Pages 1–3 photograph: Northeastern University Inter-Faith Spiritual Center by Dan Bibb
Page 143 photograph: Office dA by Jennifer Cho

Graphic Design: Lucas H. Guerra/Oscar Riera Ojeda
Layout: Oscar Riera Ojeda

CONTENTS

Foreword

BY GRAHAM OWEN

BETWEEN LANGUAGE AND MATTER: THE WORK OF OFFICE DA

The work of Office dA presents itself in this volume primarily in the form of drawings, models, and texts; in short, a project portfolio. In this respect, it would not be dissimilar to the production of a number of "young American" teacher–critics for whom academic recognition by means of the image is a primary career goal. Yet the *oeuvre* of Office dA distinguishes itself from these practices by the intensity of the desire it embodies for the "real" of building. Laden with the promise of a prodigious and compelling constructed presence, it charts a course—albeit an astutely selective one—through contemporary concerns with language, matter, and event, engaging as it travels the related, and urgent, issues of urbanity, identity, and the production of culture.

As former students and collaborators of Rodolfo Machado and Jorge Silvetti, the principals of Office dA[1] share a number of foundational concerns with that practice. These concerns have already been thoroughly and eloquently explored elsewhere by others,[2] and it would be redundant to reexamine them here. "Criticism from within," "unprecedented realism," "emergent types," "*mise-en-architecture*," "polygraphic excess," the architecturalization of infrastructure (to borrow some of the critical categories that have been deployed): all these can be found to characterize the work of Office dA as well. Closely informed by the project of structuralism, the work of Machado and Silvetti finds a willing fellow traveler in the production of their younger counterparts. Even so, as the principals of Office dA pursue the independence of position that the firm deserves, some aspects of their influential mentors' stance have receded from the foreground.

To some extent, this has to do with the changed context in which Office dA operates as a young firm. For Machado and Silvetti at the beginning of their career, seeking to establish a polemical beachhead in the theater of the 1970s, the overbearing presence in professional practice of scientistic functionalism and corporate formalism, bolstered by the fashionability of design methodology in the academies of the time, constituted a ready target for their Paris-honed intellectual weaponry. Now, more than twenty years on, those battles have been won and lost again, and the forces in the field have re-arrayed themselves in sometimes unfamiliar configurations. Machado and Silvetti, in addition to becoming builders of significance, have continued to make lucid and incisive contributions to contemporary architectural thought.[3] Nonetheless, the projects of Office dA are more cautious about declarations on the uses of history, or on the significance of type, aware as the principals are of the prize of radicalism that was so closely contested among recent would-be avant-gardes and the promiscuity with which charges of conservatism were bestowed. Similarly, Office dA concerns itself less with explicit assertions of the role of pleasure in architecture, or of erotic themes, areas in which Machado and Silvetti made notable counter-advances against the orthodoxies of their day.

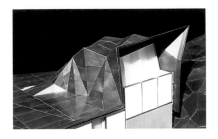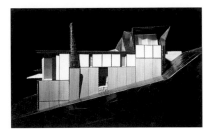

More immediate among Office dA's concerns are the counter-arguments presented in recent years to the structuralist/linguistic model by materialist–tectonic practices, and the equally assertive claims for recognition by proponents of a renewed attention to program and to science (in this case, "new science"). To the language-based model of architectural discourse that was founded upon structuralism, valorizing epistemological concerns, materialist–tectonic practices propose a counterclaim for the ontological basis of architectural value and seek a pre-linguistic response. In turn, new science advocates focus upon the event-surface as a paradigm for architecture, embracing program not as the algorithmic determinant of form but as a calculus of flows, fostering the unpredictable and predicating its form upon a particulate model of the subject. Office dA seeks to position itself—to use the title of one of its own self-descriptions—"between scenography and tectonics": between a theatrical understanding of the role of architecture as a setting for action, foregrounding the artifice of that setting's conceptual construction, and a concern for the haptic experience of physical construction as an ur-form of authenticity. [4] A precarious position, and indeed a contradictory one; but, in Office dA's hands, a productive one, and a space in which they advance a particular understanding of the subject in relation to events.

In this portfolio, Mónica Ponce de León and Nader Tehrani follow a trajectory that is in some ways opposite to the traditional sequence of a new practice, from the domestic to the public. Their remarkable, and duly recognized, project for Miami, "Public Infrastructure for the Tropics" of 1991–93, addressed issues of public space and infrastructure planning, while their more recent work has included the intensely articulate and memorable Mill Road House, Casa la Roca, Suchart House, and Zahedi House (1994, 1995, 1996, and 1998 respectively). Writing of the Suchart House, its designers note their interest in allowing figure and frame, construct and context to infiltrate each other: the library, a mimetic rock-room, is one example. This blurring of figure and frame might also be understood at the level of architectural discourse, in that these recent projects demonstrate a capacity to absorb and re-present elements of their discursive context. That this process constitutes a kind of intertextuality bears witness to the continuing pertinence of the language model for Office dA; that these absorptions and representations take place within a robust conceptual construct suggests their ambition to redirect the advances of the ontological model of tectonics.

Consider, for example, the cladding of the Mill Road House: The clapboard/louvered skin transforms itself from background vernacular texture (a guarantee of regional propriety) to seductive veil. Its gauzy modesty mediates the presence of the glass house within; the skin, then, simultaneously and with devious skill pays homage to and co-opts the famous copper wrapping of Jacques Herzog and Pierre de Meuron's Signal Box auf dem Wolf. Less directly, the presence of the Swiss firm upon Office dA's recent horizons can also be detected in the plan of the Suchart House itself, in some ways reminiscent of the Casa Koechlin, in Basel, of 1993–94. I draw attention to these affiliations not to raise doubts over authorial authenticity (an issue that must, after all, be seen as having conclusively reestablished its presence with Frank Gehry's Bilbao Guggenheim), but rather to suggest

a strategic intent on the part of Office dA: to interpolate these other architectures into a dialogical frame that reasserts the possibility and value of the actively interpreting, cognizing subject.

Consider too, as an extension of this ambition, the explorations of the "performative repertoire" of matter in Casa la Roca: *all the things that terra cotta can do.* Subjected to an encyclopedic choreography, fired clay exemplifies a tectonic theme; but not *only* a tectonic theme, as the terra cotta's performance also constitutes a response to the exigencies of site and landscape. Architecture *performs* to ameliorate and capitalize upon those exigencies, yet still to assert architecture's presence rather than defer to landscape as virtuous nature or as spectacle ("tectonic radicalization"). In demonstrating this repertoire, materials (terra cotta, at least) are nonetheless called upon to perform outside their "natural" capacities: the east wall presents itself as Semperian textile, hypothetically capable of being "drawn" back along its own curtain-rail. In the project's accompanying text, a positioning is asserted between critical regionalism (implicitly conservative as regards cognition and identity of place) and the house as a work of art (implicitly unrecognizable as domestic). A comparable positioning may be discerned once again between language and matter: in extending the range of its performative repertoire beyond pure presence into allusion and metaphor, the primary material of Casa la Roca insists on the cognitive role of the subject, a role beyond that of pure perception. This role is equally demanded, both for Casa la Roca and for the Mill Road House, in an engagement with the question of architecture's role in engendering cultural identity.

The subject's continuing cognitive engagement and performance in this engenderment is an assumption already evident in the earlier projects of urbanism. In "Miami: Public Infrastructure for the Tropics," Office dA asserts, in a series of projects of compelling depth and plausibility, its commitment to the physical and therefore the social continuity of the city, its faith in the continuing possibility of physical contiguity and community. Thus, implicitly, the Miami project asserts a resistance to the postmodern sublime, and to a concurrent attitude to urban infrastructure, the *laissez-faire* position of Rem Koolhaas and OMA. In the hands of Office dA, infrastructure is susceptible to re-figuration as monumental public artifact or space: the auto/monument becomes the monument, but *fluctuates.* This fluctuation is what inhibits the appearance of the utopian, as simply the opposite extreme of the dystopian condition conventionally associated with late twentieth-century infrastructure, exacerbated in some versions of the *laissez-faire* approach. This fluctuation is also the condition of acceptance of this infrastructure as having long duration, as distinct from the official approach taken to Boston's Central Artery: an elevated expressway understood as urbanistically aberrant and obsolete, warranting massive reinvestment to replace. Finally, the new slate "skin" of the 836 Overpass, particular and precise in its materiality and detailing, can be understood as introducing rhetorical tropes: analogy, hyperbole, metonymy. Subject to oscillating readings as fish/alligator/*opus reticulatum*, the Overpass fluctuates between the regionally natural and the architecturally and infrastructurally artificial.

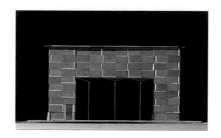

In the earlier project for the Roxbury Community Center, Office dA proposes an even clearer conjunction among language, matter, and event. Urbanity is here seen as an activity to be catalyzed by the provision of programmatically non-specific but provocative settings. The tables, large and small, constitute multivalent forms, and not only in the earlier Jencksian sense.[5] Here they suggest multiple forms of performance, invoking anew the Saussurian notion of *langue* and parole. This foundational linguistic association notwithstanding, the performative multivalence of the small tables nonetheless depends upon their material specificity as floating fragments of the recognizable concrete ground of the sidewalk. Again, drawings and models of extraordinary quality and intensity serve as a means of persuasion in the proposition of an "unprecedented urbanity": in the absence of the persuasiveness of the recognizable antecedent, or its invocation of an urbanistic collective unconscious, construction is invoked as a means to manifest the ambiguous artifact, the enigmatic monument. This approach to the urban event should be distinguished from the more etiolated renditions of New Urbanism in that the latter present an unambiguous image of what is recognizable as having been experienced, historically, as urbane. In such renditions, urbane (or at least civic) behavior is expected to be elicited in part unselfconsciously by form, but also to a significant extent as self-conscious decorum. The Roxbury Community Center, by contrast, through its deftly choreographed rapprochement between the linguistic and the material, is intended to catalyze the unselfconscious performance of the urbane event by an engaged and knowing subject, and this performance may include the unforeseen. Unprecedented urbanity may still appear, Office dA contends, by virtue of the active interpretations engaged in by the singular agent: particular, not particulate, and one whose collective vision of the city could be willed rather than a phenomenon of emergence. This contention invites participation, implying as it does the continued possibility of action in a world of market flows.

Office dA is now beginning to build, and although the initial constructions are modest in size, this *oeuvre* as a whole continues to provoke an intense desire for its tantalizing promise of the yet-to-be-experienced, and for its own performance in the realm of the material.

1. From 1986 to 1991, Rodolphe el-Khoury and Nader Tehrani were partners in Office dA, working on residential projects, with el-Khoury inclining more toward the theoretical dimension of design and Tehrani toward form and representation. With el-Khoury's entry into doctoral studies, Monica Ponce de León's involvement in the practice increased, and el-Khoury's role tended more toward that of advisor and critic. Nonetheless, all three collaborated directly on the Souks of Beirut Competition, Four Proposals for Beirut, and the Murr Tower (with Machado Silvetti), and subsequent design work reflects, they feel, their collective concerns, discussions, and background. **2.** See K. Michael Hays, ed., *Unprecedented Realism: The Architecture of Machado and Silvetti* (New York: Princeton Architectural Press, 1995). **3.** See, for example, "Afterword" in *Unprecedented Realism*. **4.** Here I refer to the more common interpretation of tectonics. **5.** Charles Jencks, *Modern Movements in Architecture* (Harmondsworth: Penguin, 1973).

Introduction

BY RODOLPHE EL-KHOURY

THE IRRESISTIBLE CHARM OF OFFICE DA

Cutler: It's about the skin, an old idea that is cleverly done.

Jimenez: We're seduced by surface manipulation. There is a joy in the fabrication of the surfaces.

Hadid: It's a prop. The skin is like a temporary structure. It's like a house wearing an inexpensive dress. You can take it off and on, change it in time, The architect puts too much emphasis on the skin; it is disposable.

Hanganu: It's a trick, but a nice trick, to take the undulated metal and perforate it, which changes the materiality and makes it transparent.

Kennedy: I think the project is about image and iconography. I wish the details they showed were actually crucial for making the project. It purports to be about tectonic issues and materials, and I'm not sure it really is. It's about image. My second concern is the back of the house. I would be enthusiastic about this project if it was all about skin and how it moves from the inside to the outside—a body wrap. But there's a loose arbitrary addition. This is a highly sophisticated project aesthetically. But the house itself, in terms of rooms, is completely conventional. *Architecture*, April 1998

Office dA received a Progressive Architecture Award in 1998 for the Weston House. The jury's comments above give a fair idea of the standard reception of the work. It is typically ambivalent. The work's power is acknowledged, but not without some reservation: the jurors bestow the award but are compelled to express a concomitant disapproval or justify their choice in quasi-apologetic terms. When the skepticism is not overt, words like "sophisticated," "clever," "seduced," or "trick" hint at the architecture's deceitful charm, the critics' unwholesome indulgence.

The ambivalence is symptomatic of a pervasive attitude: an equal dissatisfaction with the drab iconoclasm of orthodox modernism and the frivolous rhetoric of Post-Modernism. Office dA's projects suggest an intermediate course of action, "between language and matter," to use Graham Owen's formulation. The stock reactions to these proposals, whether in guilty approbation or reluctant condemnation, distill the tendencies of the current architectural debate and thus compel me to offer additional commentary. My aim is define the general terms of the debate as much as clarify Office dA's particular position. If my remarks seem biased, it is because I was a former member of the Office dA team; my interest in the work, its familiar past, and its promising future is more than academic.

The architect puts too much emphasis on the skin; it is disposable. The polemics of the surface have kept two generations of critics busy since Post-Modernism's jubilant experiments in semiotics and later, through the postmodern infatuation with surface effects. Robert Venturi and Mark Wigley may have their differences but they concur in their profound appreciation of the superficial.

Theories of the surface have indeed been treated extensively and may very well be the most significant contribution to recent architectural criticism. There is no point in rehearsing here the lessons of Las Vegas and Nietzsche except to point out Office dA's own contribution to this line of research and reopen, at least momentarily, a debate that has apparently been closed, perhaps prematurely.

Judging from the *Architecture* jury's comments, it would seem that the proverbial pendulum of history has gone full swing and that the surface is again suspect, its legitimacy as a privileged site of architectural value questioned. It is in short "disposable." The accusations are familiar; they have effectively served the modernist denigration of ornament with customary references to fashion, to the accessory and the feminine. Déjà vu? Are we dealing here with some curious cultural amnesia or perhaps a full-fledged modernist backlash?

Populist investments in surface may simply have been too vulgar and the post-structuralist kind too arcane to merit serious and lasting attention. Granted, the mere existence of the Piazza d'Italia is reason enough to justify the moratorium on "façade." But what about Herzog and de Meuron? They have built an entire career on ingenious and skillful surface treatments; they seldom fail to seduce traditionalists and avant-gardists alike and have yet to exhaust their creative potential in reinventing the elevation.

And whatever happened to the feminist/post-structuralist critique of the ornament? Already forgotten or never heard in the first place? Wigley recently demonstrated how white paint, the most immaterial of building revetments, was indispensable to the project of modern architecture. He may argue how whiteness, while representing the erasure of ornament, still functioned as a necessary ornamental substitute, but none of this will keep the Zaha Hadids from dismissing a whole building envelope as a "disposable" accessory.

Hadid's disdain for accessory cladding is all the more intriguing when provoked by a renovation project such as Office dA's Weston House: a project that by definition consists in supplementing an existing structure with new features, a design that is ostensibly most successful in integrating the new features into the existing framework. In fact, the consistency and coherence of the reclad house is such that an unsuspecting viewer would be hard-pressed to ever distinguish the skeletal ghost of the original.

The project in question is a renovation and addition to a suburban house in Weston, Massachusetts, a wood-frame building from the 1950s conforming to conventional typology, both in matters of construction and iconography. The new design calls for a strategic redistribution of the room layout and circulation with intent on maximizing the programmatic potentials of the building with minimal alterations to the structural frame. A garage, which also functions as greenhouse, is an important new feature. Its glass-clad facets are coordinated with the "draped metal forms of the house itself," in a composition of contrasting effects.

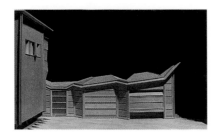

The new garage is furthermore integrated planimetrically: Its crystalline geometry extends into the house to reorganize the central hall and the vertical circulation into a smooth sequence of perspectival effects. But the *pièce de résistance* in this renovation is a new envelope, which transforms the external appearance of the house as much as the nature and quality of the living spaces within.

Short of total demolition and reconstruction, any renovation project has to deal—more or less self-consciously—with its accessory nature, with the fact that it is an add-on to an autonomous building. In the Weston House, no external traces are left of the old structure and no discernable seams lay bare the devices of the architectural "makeover." There are no attempts to represent the former autonomy (structural and formal) of the building, say by orchestrating a dialogue between old and new components. The original structure may still be supporting the roof but it is totally masked—and subsumed—by the new features.

And this is precisely why the design is an offense to modernist orthodoxy: because it allows the supplement to overwhelm the structure and make reality a function of appearance. Far from being disposable, the new cladding represents the very essence of this house. Office dA may have designed only a "dress," to use the jury's term, but this dress substantiates the clothed body; there is no body, no architecture independent of the dress.

To invest so much in the superficial accessory, to give it a structural role in defining architectural character and identity, to therefore suggest that architecture is, in a major way, a function of cladding is typical of Office dA's work but also characteristic of a wide range of postmodern practices. The distinguishing factor in Office dA's work is the investigation of the surface as a primary field of construction: building as a function of cladding. In this capacity Office dA is more in tune with Gottfried Semper's theories than Venturi's. The surface is not applied to a pre-existing solid wall as a symbolic or linguistic veneer. It is understood and designed as a constitutive spatial element as much as a vehicle to architectural and cultural signification. For Office dA, both space and language are an effect of surface constructions.

 "It purports to be about tectonic issues and materials, and I'm not sure it really is. It's about image." "Tectonics" is one of those catch-all terms that can evoke a wide range of ideas and align with different, if not contradictory ideologies. Perhaps because of this resilient ambiguity and a convoluted—if not confusing—genealogy in architectural theory, tectonics can be now found at the core of a building mythology that is keen on anchoring architectural value in the "pure presence" of building matter.

Largely in reaction to the structuralist/post-structuralist infatuation with the free-floating signifier and the indeterminacy of meaning, the cult of architectural authenticity undermines "representation" in the pursuit of some onto-mystico-metaphysical

presence or "presentation." Its rhetoric is fueled by Heideggerian clichés that architects have found particularly resonant in their allegorical reference to building and dwelling. What results is an iconoclastic brand of architectural criticism that persists on building a whole theoretical edifice on the precarious distinction between what is apparent and what is real—among other binary oppositions that phenomenology, ironically, had set to undermine.

According to the gospel of authenticity, issues of iconography, of language and rhetoric, are secondary—if not inconsequential—to essential matters of materiality and fabrication. Hence the current profusion of statements that all too readily contrast "image" and "tectonics," as if their mutual antipathy is a self-evident truth.

Yet one of the most productive themes in Office dA's work is the intersection of rhetoric and fabrication. Consistently, the detail is the field where the actual and the visible are reinvented in unexpected alliances that push both the material and method of construction to unprecedented limits.

Consider for instance "Fabricating Coincidences," an installation commissioned by New York's Museum of Modern Art for an exhibition showcasing issues of fabrication. It was constructed—with indispensable assistance from CAD/CAM technology—from sheets of steel that were creased, pleated, and folded into an elaborate sculptural form. The detail here speaks eloquently of the method of construction. Like a genetic code, it encapsulates the artifact's morphological structure and demonstrates the process of its realization. "Tell-tale details" of the sort are sanctioned by "tectonicism," never mind the fact that the overall image of the artifact hyperbolizes the process of fabrication in a quasi-rococo composition of pleated facets that puts Issey Miyaki to shame. Things get a bit thorny when the anamorphic feature of the piece is considered, when an optical agenda displaces the work to the "suspect" realm of the image.

Viewed from a designated station across MoMA's sculpture garden, the installation momentarily collapses into a flat plane. This singular optical event is an integral component of the piece and in many ways a generative factor in the design. The geometry and tectonics of the artifact were elaborated in the anticipation of this visual illusion, which simultaneously contradicts and reinforces the material and constructional principle of the detail. Here, image, geometry, material, and fabrication process are coordinated into a tense hybrid of tactile and optical effects. Does the optical rhetoric of the piece—which proves to be constitutive—and its dematerialized representation of flatness compromise the soundness of its so-called tectonics? Or, on the contrary, does the particular tectonic quality of the piece emerge from the contrived tension between fact and illusion, between what is represented and what is presented, between the image and the material structure?

Another fact will complicate this picture even more: The rigidity of the steel facets is not entirely due to the fold; a camouflaged conventional beam provides additional support and stiffness. Camouflage consists here in a staggered contour that allows the beam to be "smuggled" in the fold. In a true camouflage manner, the artifice is simultaneously revealed and concealed: The beam is visible and the logic of stealth intelligible. The architects draw you into the tectonic representation of the fold with a complex and ambivalent visual device. They count on the visual to complement rather than merely present the actual performance of the detail. What things *look as though they are doing* is as important as what they are *actually doing.*

Such artifice, whether entirely concealed or deliberately laid bare, is bound to put off the mainstream tectonicists; their purism will tolerate neither sham nor rhetoric. Yet any experienced practitioner will recognize the artifice for what it really is: a mere trick of the trade. Germain Soufflot had much use for it in Sainte-Geneviéve—one of the first self-consciously modern monument where issues of tectonics were paramount. Hidden arches and elaborate steel reinforcement here assist, covertly, in demonstrating the tectonic verity of the freestanding column and the simple rectilinear beam, the constitutive elements of Soufflot's Gothic-inspired architecture. The building is most valued as a quintessential illustration of Rationalist structural principles; never mind that despite its copious provision of stealth supports, the building would have long collapsed without a battery of additional tricks.

Speaking of the Gothic, what would the tectonicist make of flying buttresses? They are ostensibly designed to sustain a structural illusion within the nave, an image of lightness and effortlessness that is contradictory to their prodigious display of structural gymnastics outside. Epitome of tectonic expression or shameless visual deception? Consider the possibility, daringly suggested by Erwin Panofsky, that the stone vaults did not always require additional bracing, that the flying buttress was a matter of rhetoric as much as statics. The flying buttress—so dear to a Violet Leduc—would be tricking us into thinking that it is performing a structural trick. Two-fold illusion; double heresy?

This much is clear: Image and tectonics are far from enemies, and Office dA capitalizes on their complicity. Instances where the optical logic of the image permeates the haptic principles of construction are indeed a staple of Office dA; they are perhaps the firm's most consistent and original contribution to the poetics of building. The curtain-wall of the Weston House performs accordingly and accounts for much of the building's appeal. Consider also the garden wall of Casa la Roca: The undulating filigree of bricks is designed to provide a thin free-standing wall with structural integrity, but the visual impression is one of fragility and dramatic instability. And, as if the contradiction between structural material and visual effect were not enough of a heresy, the overall image of a drawn curtain adds a quasi-Surrealist touch of dematerialization.

"This is a highly sophisticated project aesthetically. But the house itself, in terms of rooms, is completely conventional." Most of Office dA's buildings have conventional plans. They are conventional in their predominantly orthogonal geometry and in their conformity to established types. This is evidently the case in renovation/appropriation projects in which the architects had to operate within pre-existing frameworks, but also true of new structures where ostensibly benign plans seldom convey the flagrant inventiveness of the spaces they create.

There is no accident in Office dA's interest in transforming existing structures: They allow the architects to rely exclusively on sectional and elevational strategies as a means to complement and transcend the pragmatic contingencies of the plan. The Inter-Faith Chapel is a case in point: The cladding strategy (including floor, wall, and ceiling revetments) transforms a standard windowless room that is accessed from an institutional corridor into an otherworldly luminescent space: totally unexpected and far from conventional as a spatial phenomenon; still your run-of-the-mill rectangular room in plan. The design for the Murr Tower performs analogous operations on a concrete monolith, this time with exterior cladding and virtually no alterations to the plan.

The Miami Overpass project also exemplifies Office dA's mode of operation: The new surfaces transform a merely functional piece of equipment into a public space that presents a convincing potential for the revitalization of a whole district. Once again, the design strategy overlays a whole new dimension to the structure without ever disturbing its planimetric and functional logic. Barely recognizable in its reinvented section, the new hybrid structure speaks, perhaps most eloquently, of the transformative—and redemptive—power of the surface.

Hence the design ambition behind the cladding strategy of the Weston House: "While the corrugated metal is wrapped around the existing house as a thin drape, it is also called on to re-formulate the idea, perception and space of the house." But in situations in which Office dA is not presented with existing structures for its redemptive process, the tendency is to rely on types or straightforward planimetric configurations to set up conventional frameworks for highly unusual phenomena. The device is tactical: The "ready-made" plan embodies the conventional and pragmatic aspects of building-for-everyday-life that are challenged by the unorthodox surface. The tension between planimetric expectations and sectional inventions yields a highly defamiliarized spatial experience, which accommodates and exceeds the commonplace.

What I have described is a general tendency and certainly not a constant in Office dA's work. There are instances where the transformative tension is played out differently, among other conflicting features of the project. For instance, the Suchart House

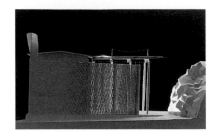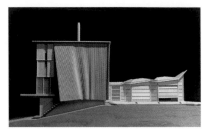

confronts typological abstraction with symbolic figuration "by allowing the figure to infiltrate and occasionally subvert the frame." What is consistent is the (transformative) redemptive process that is built into the structure of the design: A conventional platform accommodates the mundane aspects of dwelling and provides a springboard for their transfiguration in design.

There is a pragmatic logic—and an implicit political agenda—in Office dA's design strategy, which merits some attention. The pragmatism is most evident in domestic programs where conventional room layouts are streamlined for customization through inhabitation. The "weak form" of the generic plan can accommodate standard furnishings and is most amenable to individuated lifestyles and decorative whims. Of the political, suffice it now to mention that when CAD/CAM technology makes "total design" an economically competitive option, Office dA's insistence on setting the particular within the generic is a function of ideology as much as of practicality.

A colleague related to me an incident that took place while he was serving on a jury for a prestigious architectural award. About to enter one of the buildings that was short-listed for the first prize, he was stopped by an attendant who denied him access because of his shoes. This evidently brings to mind Adolf Loos' parody of Jugendstile, "The Famous Story of the Poor Rich Man" where an overzealous architect tyrannically controlled every aspect of his total design, down to the slippers of his intimidated client. In the case at hand, however, the footwear was delinquent in matters of security rather than style. Apparently, the ramping floors of the building, designed to demonstrate the aesthetic and programmatic virtues of folded space, have proven to be treacherously slippery. After several mishaps with unsuspecting visitors, the insurance company dictated the use of rubber-soled shoes within the premises. The building evidently did not fare well with the juror who, after exchanging his fine English shoes for the courtesy-to-visitors-Adidas, was ill-disposed for the leap of faith that avant-garde architecture so stubbornly demands. The virtues of the warped field and the architect's theories of emancipatory space—or was it the critique of capitalist flows?—left him cold.

Clearly no such challenges, intellectual or physical, are posed by the Weston House—or any other house by Office dA, for that matter. No ban on stiletto-heeled pumps; no claims for the deconstruction of ideological closure. The Weston House may be "a highly sophisticated project aesthetically," but it is still a house. Obviously, this is not a "completely conventional" house because the architects, while knowing where to tactically—and tactfully—conform to certain norms of building and habitation, also exploit the many opportunities for invention that do not impose tyrannical demands (financial, practical, or experiential) on the users. The demonstration of formal and technological ingenuity is unmistakable and far from conventional, say in the corner treatment, but that will not keep the living spaces from agreeing with IKEA furniture.

Office dA's tactics are clearly demonstrated in Casa la Roca: innovation is most radical in the sculptural garden wall extending from the main body of the house. When architecture is here released, physically and symbolically, from its more mundane domestic duties, it can assume more aesthetically ambitious aims, ones that are rightfully held within the reach of art.

So when Mónica Ponce de León and Nader Tehrani are commissioned to create an installation for an exhibition at MoMA—a bona fide work of art—they are not shy of theoretical and formal exuberance. And even rubber soles will not protect museum-goers from razor-sharp edges and treacherous trompe-l'oeil should they foolishly brave the bizarre stairs the two concocted for the occasion.

The term *convenance*, inadequately translated as "decorum," comes loaded with wearisome allusions to stuffy Ancien-Regime codes of propriety and may be hopelessly antiquated. Yet, with some measure of adaptation, it may very well be suited to describe Office dA's ability to tactically calibrate the tone and intensity of their designs to suit particular cultural and material circumstances— and I am obviously not talking about iconography nor contextualism.

This ostensibly rudimentary faculty, which requires some measure of judgment—and a great deal of restraint—currently seems to be blunted, especially in avant-garde practices. Office dA's work eloquently demonstrates how a keener sense of *convenance* can do much to sharpen the wit and poignancy of architectural invention.

Built Work ▶

Fabrications: The Tectonic Garden, "Fabricating Coincidences"

Ostensibly pertaining to the act of making, building, and manufacturing, the concept of "fabrication" is also connected to fabric and weaving, to notions of deceit, forgery, and fiction. It is with these complex and sometimes divergent references that Office dA approaches "fabrication," the theme of the MoMA exhibition—and the central preoccupation of the firm's work, in general. The installation is accordingly ambiguous; it works with folded-steel-plate technology as a way of blurring the traditional distinctions between structure and skin, supporting and supported building elements. Triangulation gives the steel skin rigidity, while folded columnar plates give the structure lateral bracing. This geometry is also developed on optical and anamorphic principles, yielding particular spatial readings from different points of view. The form of the installation and its relationship with the museum wall are furthermore designed to suggest different uses and modes of inhabitation, above and below the steel plate: stair; canopy, bleacher, shelter—not to mention sculpture, and even painting. The structure accommodates for material, spatial and programmatic variations in continuous and seamless adaptations, underplaying the normative tectonic articulation of difference. For instance, variations in the density of the perforations lighten the steel structure as it unfolds upward, allowing the gradual passage of light to the space beneath. While steel construction is customarily predicated on a trabeated system of T-sections, angles, and I-beams, this installation devises an alternative system in which steel is stretched and stitched like fabric. Warps, creases, and folds in a continuous structural surface substitute here for the traditional beam and column and effectively accommodate for different load and support conditions.

The project was initially conceived and drafted manually. Nevertheless, its development toward fabrication depended on the use of the computer, especially in its direct connection to the manufacturing process. Perforating, laser-cutting, and "stitching" were the three fabrication techniques translated directly from the computer files. The perforation involved a punching process that calibrated precisely the gradation of density throughout the steel surface. The outline of each steel piece was finely laser-cut so as to minimize the usual tolerance required in a construction process. The folds were achieved through a process termed "stitching," a technique that has never been tested at this scale and with this gauge of metal. Instead of bending plates of steel or welding different pieces of steel together—which would result in far less precision or a larger radius on each bend—the pieces of steel are scored by laser in an offset pattern. The outcome is a continuous twisted seam at the fold of each plate, producing the illusion of a stitch between two pieces of fabric.

The consistent aim was to avoid fabrication from an assembly of discrete constituent parts and devise a tectonic of seamlessness: a system that can absorb and deploy a heterogeneous set of informants and effects. Office dA thinks of it as "fabricating coincidences," a process where issues of structure, program, lighting, and cladding are coordinated and reconciled in a continuous, homogeneous, but differentiated surface.

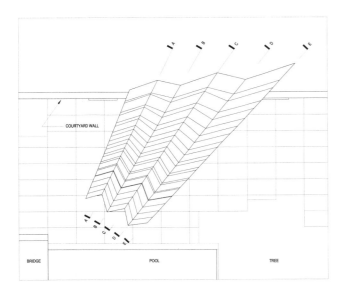

PLAN

(This Page) Views of installation peeking over the garden wall toward 54th Street.

(This Page) Views of installation from various vantage points in the garden. (Opposite Page) View of installation from station point where anamorphic flatness is achieved. (Following Spread) View of installation from underneath, exposing wrapped flanges and buttress connections.

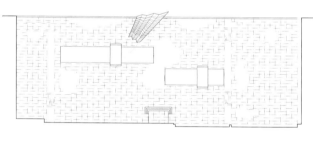

SITE PLAN

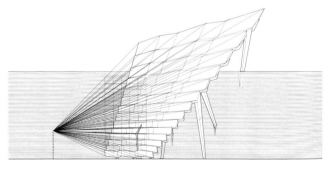

COURTYARD ELEVATION

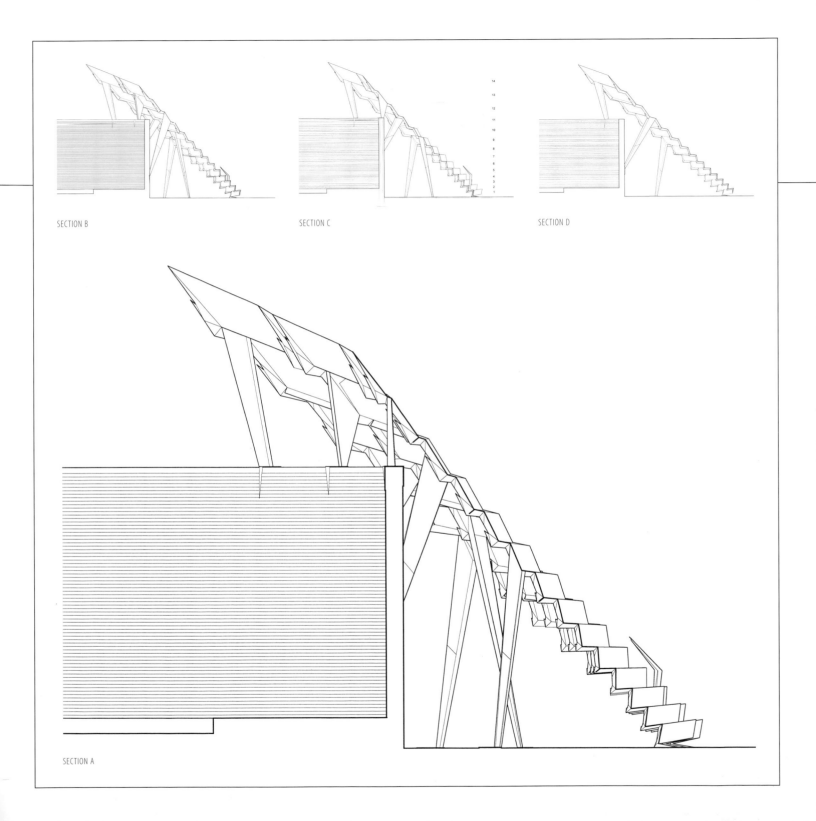

SECTION B

SECTION C

SECTION D

SECTION A

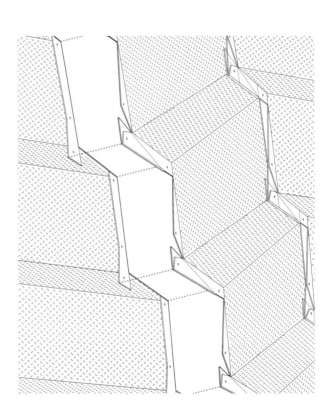

(Top Image) The steel surface is perforated at varied densities, making the installation appear transparent as it ascends. (Bottom Images) Details of tread and riser flaps wrapping around structural flanges. (Opposite Page) Detail of flaps showing stitched seams.

AXONOMETRIC VIEW DETAIL

(This Page) View of the installation's underside. (Opposite Page) Details of buttress and leg connections (center) and detail of stitched seam.

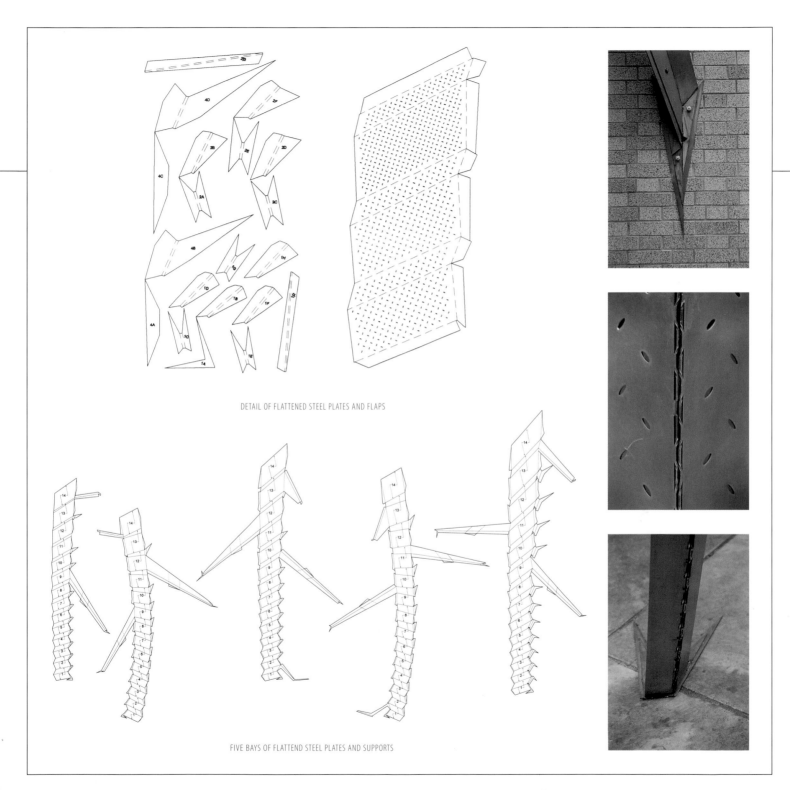

DETAIL OF FLATTENED STEEL PLATES AND FLAPS

FIVE BAYS OF FLATTEND STEEL PLATES AND SUPPORTS

Art Center College

Inter-Faith Spiritual Center

BOSTON, MASSACHUSETTS

This project was commissioned by the Northeastern University Spiritual Life Center for the renovation and rehabilitation of the University's Inter-Faith Chapel—located in the heart of the campus, on the second floor of the Ell Center. The commission epitomizes the institution's struggle with the changing character of the country's demographics: as Northeastern University became increasingly multi-cultural, the existing chapel failed to satisfy the needs of various non-Christian faith groups on campus, despite—and because of—its alleged claims of "neutrality." For instance, the chapel was oriented toward the West, precluding one of the elemental prerequisites for Islamic ritual, the orientation toward Mecca. Although the existing space did not contain specific religious icons or symbols, the functional elements of the space (pews, altar, and pulpit) were characteristic of Christian faith and encumbered other religious practices.

As part of a larger institutional building, the character of Northeastern's Inter-Faith Chapel was compromised. While most places of prayer typically enjoy a privileged position in a given context, nondenominational chapels are often a component of larger institutional or public buildings (universities, hospitals, airports) and more recently, an unlikely feature of shopping malls and office parks. As a result, the nondenominational chapel is usually conditioned by its relationship to and dependence on buildings of a secular character. Accordingly, Northeastern University's Inter-Faith Chapel lacked both a ceremonial presence and a religious character. The space was entered circumstantially from a corridor, like any other classroom in the building, without the ritualistic sequence of spaces that anticipate places of prayer or spirituality. The room itself did not have any spatial, phenomenal, or iconographic features that would distinguish it as a place of prayer; as such, the room could easily be mistaken for any lecture hall. There was no natural light—except from the corridor—and fluorescent tubes in a conventional hung ceiling supplied artificial lighting, also characteristic of institutional interiors. Other surfaces included white plaster walls and a green wall-to-wall carpet of mediocre finish.

For the proposed design, the entry into the space is modified so as to mark the ceremony of the threshold. Entry is allowed from two sides in order not to privilege any particular orientation. The space of the Spiritual Center is divided into three areas, two antechambers and the hall of prayer. To the east, a dark wood-clad space serves as a meeting room and library for books of the various faiths; it also holds the accessories needed in the rituals of various religions. The secular character of the room allows the juxtaposition of such icons without contradiction, in the museal manner. To the west, a light wood-clad space serves as an Ablution Room for the Muslim community and houses a stainless steel foot-wash. Between the two antechambers, a larger room stripped of any specific religious iconography is to be used as a "sacred" space for prayer; this room is conceived as a luminous space. The diaphanous lighting—a rhetorical feature of many religious architectures—is contrary to ones expectations in this location—at the core of the building—and should clearly differentiate the chapel from other adjacent secular spaces.

Detail of curtain wall with
cascading glass panels set
within plywood structure.

The floor is refinished in large sheets of Brazilian cherry, bordered by zinc strips, creating a monumental scale for a surface on which to pray—as used for Islamic as well as other religious rites. It is polished enough to acquire a reflective quality, consistent with the other elements of the space.

The walls are lined with layered, sandblasted glass supported by notched, laminated plywood fins and lit from behind. The cladding alters from bay to bay depending on the irregularities of the existing wall behind. Three variations are possible: Where the existing wall is in close proximity, the glass curtain-wall "drapes" to the ground, concealing the pilaster behind. Where there are niches, the glass hangs above the floor, high enough to allow access to the lighting fixtures. The curtain-wall is fully drawn in front of the entryways.

The ceiling embraces the pragmatic exigencies of the room (HVAC) and capitalizes on the modest proportions of the space to create visual drama from spatial compression. This unorthodox hung ceiling is composed of oversized vents; they are best described as a cross between an overturned pendentive dome and the diaphragm of a camera lens. Their cascading sheets of perforated aluminum loom heavy with suspended mass, light with reflected luminescence.

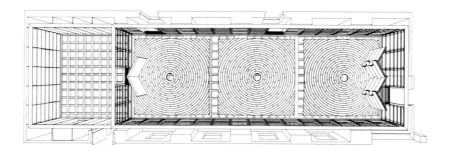

REFLECTED CEILING PERSPECTIVE

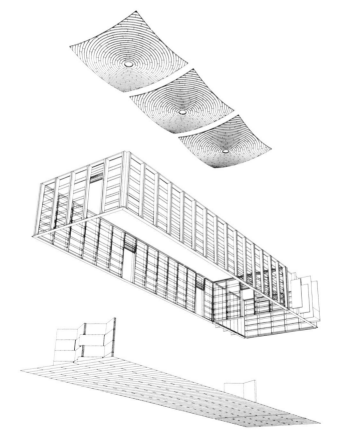

(Top) Ablution room wall and ceiling wood paneling incorporates HVAC and lighting fixtures. (Middle) Detail of laser-cut metal edge of ablution wash basin. (Bottom and Opposite) View of ablution room from main hall.

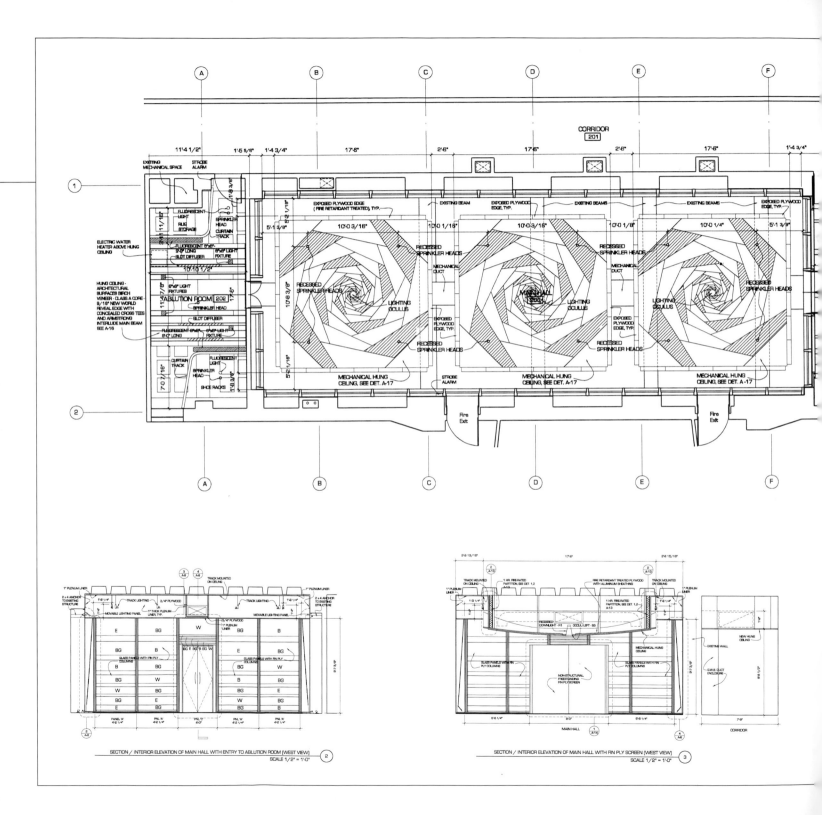

CORRIDOR
201

EXISTING MECHANICAL SPACE
STROBE ALARM

EXPOSED PLYWOOD EDGE (FIRE RETARDANT TREATED), TYP.

EXISTING BEAM

EXPOSED PLYWOOD EDGE, TYP.

EXISTING BEAMS

EXISTING BEAMS

EXPOSED PLYWOOD EDGE, TYP.

FLUORESCENT LIGHT

RUG STORAGE

SPRINKLER HEAD

CURTAIN TRACK

ELECTRIC WATER HEATER ABOVE HUNG CEILING

FLUORESCENT 8"x6" 9'-0" LONG SLOT DIFFUSER

6"x6" LIGHT FIXTURE

RECESSED SPRINKLER HEADS

RECESSED SPRINKLER HEADS

HUNG CEILING - ARCHITECTURAL SURFACES BIRCH VENEER - CLASS A CORE 9/16" NEW WORLD REVEAL EDGE WITH CONCEALED CROSS TEES AND ARMSTRONG INTERLUDE MAIN BEAM SEE A-16

ABLUTION ROOM 202

6"x6" LIGHT FIXTURES

SPRINKLER HEAD

SLOT DIFFUSER

RECESSED SPRINKLER HEADS

MECHANICAL DUCT

MAIN HALL 203

LIGHTING OCULUS

MECHANICAL DUCT

LIGHTING OCULUS

LIGHTING OCULUS

RECESSED SPRINKLER HEADS

FLUORESCENT 8"x6" 9'-0" LONG SLOT FIXTURE

CURTAIN TRACK

FLUORESCENT LIGHT

SPRINKLER HEAD

EXPOSED PLYWOOD EDGE, TYP.

EXPOSED PLYWOOD EDGE, TYP.

SHOE RACKS

MECHANICAL HUNG CEILING, SEE DET. A-17

STROBE ALARM

MECHANICAL HUNG CEILING, SEE DET. A-17

RECESSED SPRINKLER HEADS

MECHANICAL HUNG CEILING, SEE DET. A-17

Fire Exit

Fire Exit

SECTION / INTERIOR ELEVATION OF MAIN HALL WITH ENTRY TO ABLUTION ROOM (WEST VIEW) 2
SCALE 1/2" = 1'-0"

1" PLENUM LINER

TRACK MOUNTED ON CEILING

TRACK LIGHTING

2 x 4 ANCHOR TO EXISTING STRUCTURE

MOVABLE LIGHTING PANEL

3/4" PLYWOOD

1" THICK PLENUM LINER, TYP.

3/4" PLYWOOD

1" PLENUM LINER

TRACK LIGHTING

MOVABLE LIGHTING PANEL

2 x 4 ANCHOR TO EXISTING STRUCTURE

GLASS PANELS WITH FIN PLY COLUMNS

GLASS PANELS WITH FIN PLY COLUMNS

E	BG		W		E	BG
BG	B				BG	W
B	BG	BG E BG B BG W		BG	B
BG	W				B	BG
W	E				BG	E
BG	E				W	BG
E	BG				B	E

PANEL W | PNL B | PNL C | PNL W

SECTION / INTERIOR ELEVATION OF MAIN HALL WITH FIN PLY SCREEN (WEST VIEW) 3
SCALE 1/2" = 1'-0"

TRACK MOUNTED ON CEILING

1" PLENUM LINER

1 HR. FIRE-RATED PARTITION, SEE DET 1,2 A-13

FIRE RETARDANT TREATED PLYWOOD WITH ALUMINUM SHEATHING

TRACK MOUNTED ON CEILING

1" PLENUM LINER

RECESSED DOWNLIGHT - R1

OCULI LIFT - B3

1 HR. FIRE-RATED PARTITION, SEE DET 1,2 A-13

MECHANICAL HUNG CEILING

GLASS PANELS WITH FIN PLY COLUMNS

NON-STRUCTURAL FREESTANDING FIN PLY SCREEN

GLASS PANELS WITH FIN PLY COLUMNS

EXISTING WALL

G.W.B. DUCT ENCLOSURE

NEW HUNG CEILING

MAIN HALL

CORRIDOR

DIFFUSER PANELS
LIGHTING FIXTURES

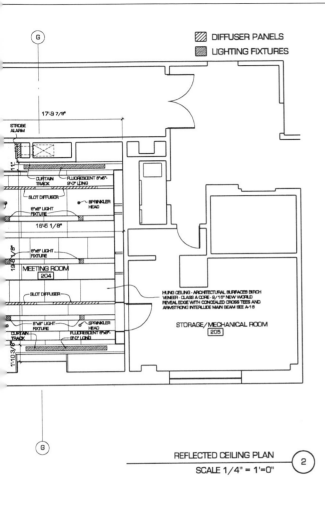

17'-9 7/8"

STROBE
ALARM

CURTAIN
TRACK

FLUORESCENT 8"x8"-
9'-0" LONG

SLOT DIFFUSER

6"x8" LIGHT
FIXTURE

SPRINKLER
HEAD

16'-5 1/8"

6"x8" LIGHT
FIXTURE

MEETING ROOM
204

SLOT DIFFUSER

HUNG CEILING - ARCHITECTURAL SURFACES BIRCH
VENEER - CLASS A CORE - 9/16" NEW WORLD
REVEAL EDGE WITH CONCEALED CROSS TEES AND
ARMSTRONG INTERLUDE MAIN BEAM SEE A-16

6"x8" LIGHT
FIXTURE

SPRINKLER
HEAD

CURTAIN
TRACK

FLUORESCENT 8"x8"-
9'-0" LONG

STORAGE/MECHANICAL ROOM
205

REFLECTED CEILING PLAN (2)
SCALE 1/4" = 1'=0"

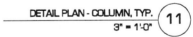
3/4" 3/4" 1/2" 1/2" 3/4" 3/4"

FIN PLY

MEMBER B2

FIRE RETARDANT
TREATED PLYWOOD

MEMBER E1

TEMPERED GLASS

1/4"

CONCEALED
GLASS SUPPORT

MEMBER B1

1" FIN PLY NOSING

2 1/2"

DETAIL PLAN - COLUMN, TYP. (11)
3" = 1'-0"

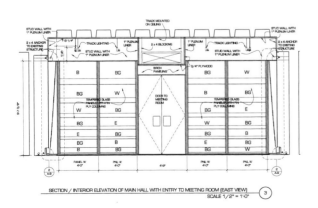

STUD WALL WITH
1" PLENUM LINER

TRACK MOUNTED
ON CEILING

STUD WALL WITH
1" PLENUM LINER

2 x 4 ANCHOR
TO EXISTING
STRUCTURE

TRACK LIGHTING

1" PLENUM
LINER

2 x 4 BLOCKING

1" PLENUM
LINER

TRACK LIGHTING

STUD WALL WITH
1" PLENUM LINER

2 x 4 ANCHOR
TO EXISTING
STRUCTURE

3/4" PLYWOOD

BIRCH
PANELING

BG

B

BG

W

B

BG

W

W

E

DOOR TO
MEETING
ROOM

BG

TEMPERED GLASS
PANELS WITH FIN
PLY COLUMNS

BG

E

TEMPERED GLASS
PANELS WITH FIN
PLY COLUMNS

BG

BG

E

W

BG

BG

B

E

BG

B

BG

B

BG

BG

W

PANEL W
4'-0"

PNL W
4'-0"

4'-0"

PNL W
4'-0"

PNL W
4'-0"

SECTION / INTERIOR ELEVATION OF MAIN HALL WITH ENTRY TO MEETING ROOM (EAST VIEW) (3)
SCALE 1/2" = 1'-0"

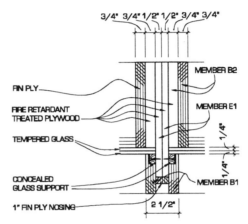

Views of main hall as furnished for different rituals. (Top) Seating for Christian faith. (Bottom) Carpets for Muslim faith.

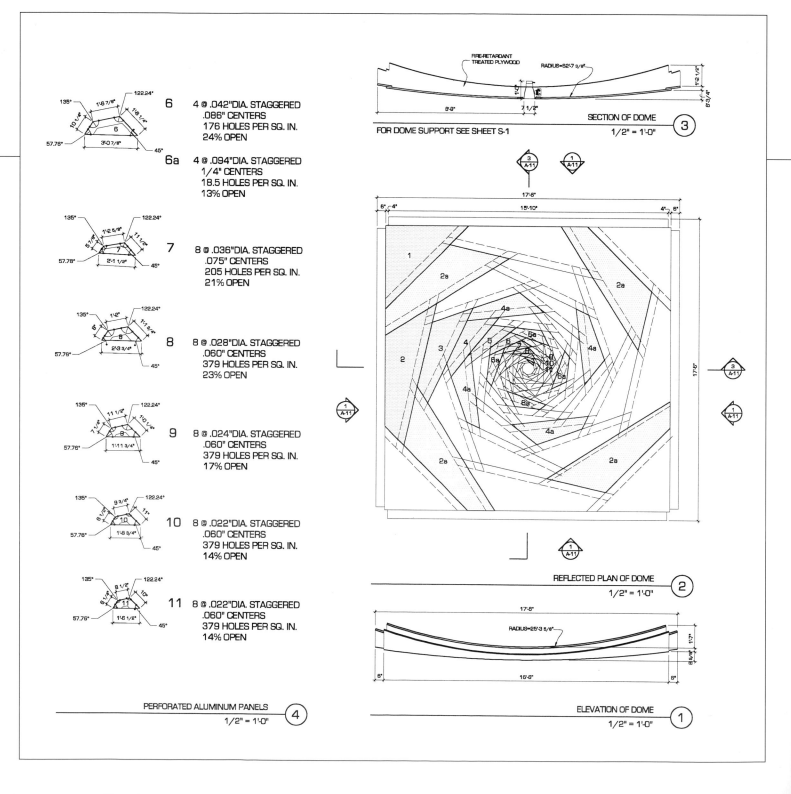

6   4 @ .042"DIA. STAGGERED
.086" CENTERS
176 HOLES PER SQ. IN.
24% OPEN

6a   4 @ .094"DIA. STAGGERED
1/4" CENTERS
18.5 HOLES PER SQ. IN.
13% OPEN

7   8 @ .036"DIA. STAGGERED
.075" CENTERS
205 HOLES PER SQ. IN.
21% OPEN

8   8 @ .028"DIA. STAGGERED
.060" CENTERS
379 HOLES PER SQ. IN.
23% OPEN

9   8 @ .024"DIA. STAGGERED
.060" CENTERS
379 HOLES PER SQ. IN.
17% OPEN

10   8 @ .022"DIA. STAGGERED
.060" CENTERS
379 HOLES PER SQ. IN.
14% OPEN

11   8 @ .022"DIA. STAGGERED
.060" CENTERS
379 HOLES PER SQ. IN.
14% OPEN

FIRE-RETARDANT
TREATED PLYWOOD

RADIUS=62'-7 5/8"

SECTION OF DOME

FOR DOME SUPPORT SEE SHEET S-1   1/2" = 1'-0"   3

REFLECTED PLAN OF DOME   2
1/2" = 1'-0"

PERFORATED ALUMINUM PANELS   4
1/2" = 1'-0"

RADIUS=25'-3 5/8"

ELEVATION OF DOME   1
1/2" = 1'-0"

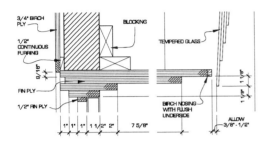

3/4" BIRCH PLY

1/2" CONTINUOUS FURRING

BLOCKING

TEMPERED GLASS

8/16"

FIN PLY

1/2" FIN PLY

BIRCH NOSING WITH FLUSH UNDERSIDE

1 1/8"

1 1/2"

ALLOW 3/8" - 1/2"

1" 1" 1 1/2" 2"   7 5/8"

DETAIL SECTION - DOOR HEAD (202) WITH PANEL C (8)
3" = 1'-0"

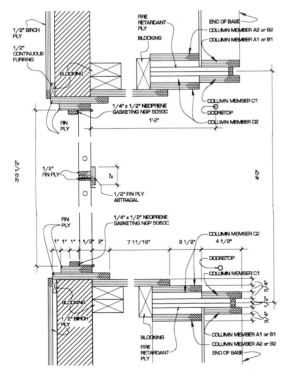

1/2" BIRCH PLY

1/2" CONTINUOUS FURRING

BLOCKING

FIN PLY

FIRE RETARDANT PLY

BLOCKING

END OF BASE

COLUMN MEMBER A2 or B2

COLUMN MEMBER A1 or B1

1/4" x 1/2" NEOPRENE GASKETING NGP 5050C

COLUMN MEMBER C1

DOORSTOP

COLUMN MEMBER C2

1'-2"

3'-3 1/2"

1/2" FIN PLY

2"

1/2" FIN PLY ASTRAGAL

4'-0"

FIN PLY

1/4" x 1/2" NEOPRENE GASKETING NGP 5050C

COLUMN MEMBER C2
4 1/2"

DOORSTOP

COLUMN MEMBER C1

1" 1" 1 1/2" 2"   7 11/16"   3 1/2"

3/4"
1/2"
3/4"

BLOCKING

1/2" BIRCH PLY

BLOCKING

FIRE RETARDANT PLY

END OF BASE

COLUMN MEMBER A1 or B1

COLUMN MEMBER A2 or B2

DETAIL PLAN - DOOR JAMB (202) WITH PANEL C (7)
3" = 1'-0"

(Opposite) Detail view of retracted glass panels at entry condition. (This Page) Base details of cascading glass. (Top) Connection between pilaster and niche condition. (Middle) Niche condition. (Bottom) Corner condition.

Oscar Riera Ojeda Furniture Collection

Part of a broader collection, the Oscar Riera Ojeda bookshelf is designed as a free-standing shelving system that is accessible from both sides. As such, it is able to yield its maximum architectural potential by behaving like a partition, a screen, or a free-standing wall in a plan-libre situation. The individual shelves are pinned to the frame so as to house books in both directions, imbuing a programmatic dimension to both sides of the frame—for instance, between a den and a living area. In standing free, the bookshelf lacks a traditional backboard that gives normative shelving the necessary structural stability against lateral forces. Herein lies the piece's most distinguishing feature: the frame of the bookshelf is fabricated from slipped laminated plywood "leaves" that wrap around the corners to create a "moment" connection in the most structurally sensitive location of the piece. The plywood is also laminated with a recessed steel strap at its core reinforcing the wood. The plywood wraps in a clockwise direction on the inside and a counter-clockwise direction on the outside in order to create the necessary slippage at its corners. The piece is finished with a dark walnut exterior and a light maple interior as a way of accentuating the opposing laminations of plywood—essentially by pointing to the darker and lighter color that veneer produces as it is stacked in perpendicular directions. The bottom corners are the most characteristic moments, because multiple wood laminations are extended, in a "shredded" fashion, to produce book-ends. The entire piece is propped up on six casters, making the shelving easily movable and flexible as partitions. Two cast aluminum handles are lodged into delaminated sections of the frame to enable the movement of the shelving unit. The design of the piece capitalizes on the tension between the tectonic logic of materials and the will to create seamless connections between functionally distinct parts of the design—for instance, at the wood corners or the junction between the steel flanges and pin-holes. Neither fully smoothed over, nor trapped in the logic of conventional construction tropes, the Oscar Riera Ojeda shelf attempts to invent new programmatic, structural, and spatial possibilities for a familiar piece of furniture.

 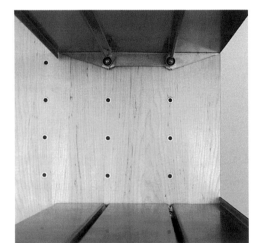 

 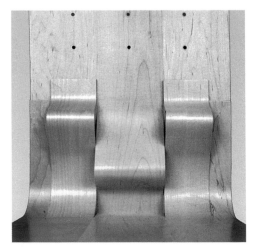 

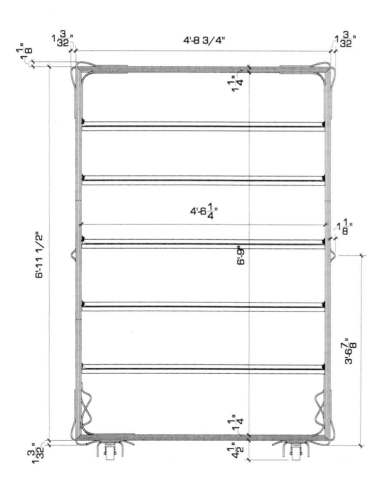

FRONT ELEVATION

(Opposite) Details of shelving corners and mid-section. (This Page) View of shelf frame exposing wrapped plywood flaps at corner conditions.

Work in Progress ▶

The Toledo House

Located in the outskirts of Bilbao, the Toledo House is in a context that typifies much of the emerging suburban condition—a world of cul-de-sacs, vehicular dominance, and a soft brand of eclecticism that caters to the public's sense of *gemutlich*. Nevertheless, the house is being built at a cultural moment that is very unique to Bilbao. After the construction of several major public projects, the Basque region is regaining a renewed political identity that is greatly indebted to architecture and urban design.

In this project, Office dA set out to develop an architectural response to the tension between the global impact of technologies and local building traditions—in effect reconciling state-of-the-art computer-aided design processes with local stone and masonry construction techniques. Interpreting an archetypal Basque building typology—the timber-framed structure with masonry infill—the proposal draws on this composite system of construction to invent new spatial, morphological, and tectonic conditions. The system uses laser-cut marine grade plywood wood members to fabricate a scaffolding structure that is incrementally filled with a "load-bearing" stone veneer and concrete block cavity wall. The scaffolding enables highly complex spatial and formal relationships and dispenses with costly customized components or processes.

The site is on a sloped hill near a cul-de-sac on a suburban tributary. Uphill views remain clear and untouched while the immediate adjacent plots have either been built or are in the process of development. The sloping site provides the opportunity to use an elevated podium for accessing distant views across the valley and beyond. The house engages the landscape in an architectural promenade that ascends the hill and travels through the building, winding up again to culminate in a public terrace and a pool. The house and landscape are woven together in a seamless fashion, blurring the traditional separation between site and building. The separation is further blurred in a rhetorical articulation of the building's solidity, evoking a massive rock set into the hill—a metaphor that capitalizes on the figurative and material qualities of stone masonry.

With some poetic license—and a mild stretch of the imagination, the Toledo house may be described as a cross between the French Hotel and the Corbusian villa: an unlikely marriage between *poché* and free plans. The plan is organized around a courtyard whose orientation brings southern light into all the major rooms of the house. The rooms defer to this principle of organization; they are accordingly rotated, fenestrated, distorted, and distributed around the court. Each room is defined as distinct spaces and forms, matching character with program in the manner of the French hotel (dining/oval, living/pinched rectangle, stair hall/triangle, study/cube, etc.)—albeit without the

(This Page) View of central hall toward living room. (Opposite) Sequence of perspectives from entry up to the roof.

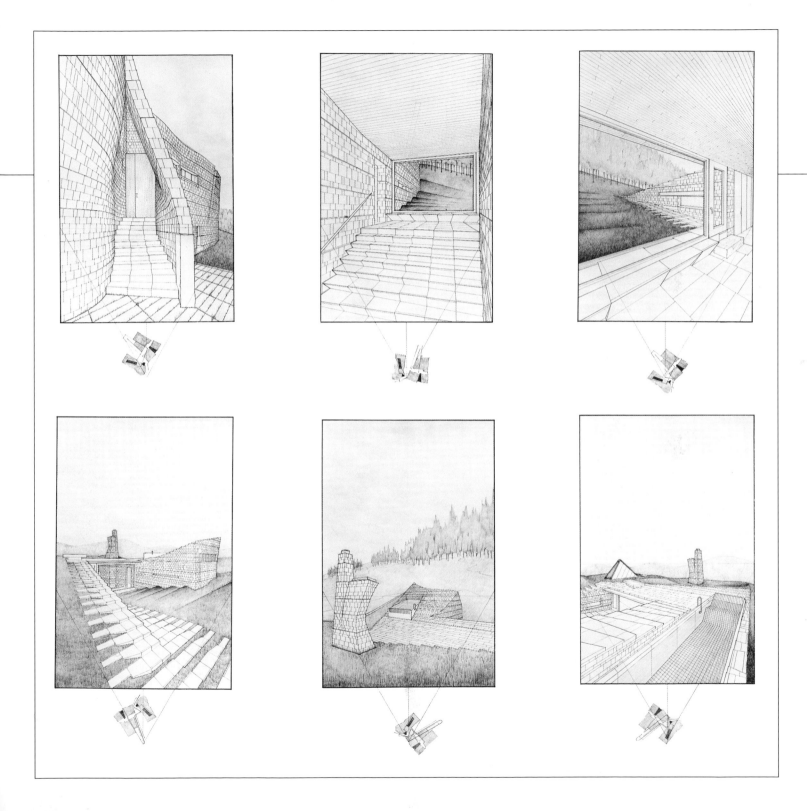

(This Page Top) West elevation.
(Bottom) Section through main
staircase. (Opposite Top Left:)
Section through secondary stair.
(Opposite Bottom Left) East
elevation. (Opposite Top Right)
Detail of roof scupper. (Opposite
Bottom Right) Detail of dining
room roof.

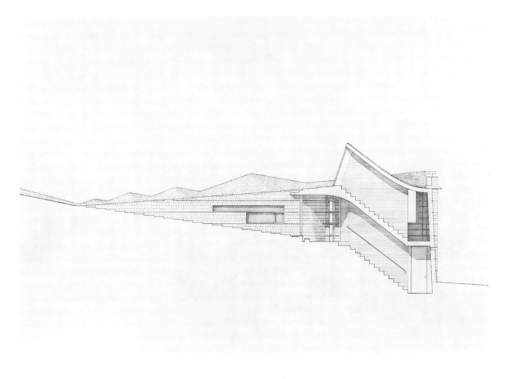

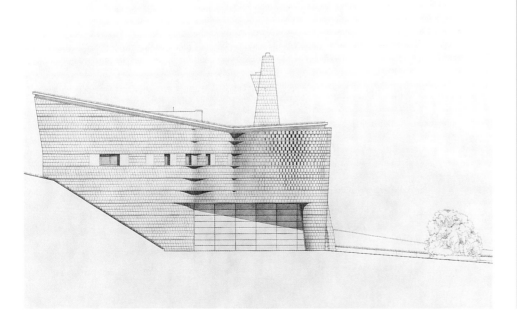

Details of structural jigs with stone infill. (Top) Dining room stone screen. (Bottom) Stone vault at main entry.

The Zahedi House

When adding onto or reconfiguring a structure, the terms of a proposal are always in tension and play with the existing features. Such is the case with the Zahedi House, a project that sets out to give a new form to an existing skeleton, capitalizing on the building's potential (its structure, circulation, and spatial properties) to reinvent itself.

While the town of Weston generally conforms to the typical American suburban condition, its density is relatively low and its meandering roads evoke the New England rural landscape. The Zahedi House typifies the picturesque qualities of the neighborhood: it sits on a hill approximately 25 feet (7.5 meters) above street level, with oblique relationships to the yard, a gently climbing driveway, and a carport nestled into the contours of the landscape. The dominant views toward and from the house consistently emphasize the corner; the new design proceeds accordingly.

The existing house is entered at the middle of a split stair, giving access to bedrooms in the basement and the living areas above. The clients wish to add an extra floor, relocating the bedrooms to the top while liberating the basement for a home office. A new stair is suspended from the second floor on axis with the existing stair, hovering over the entry sequence. Most importantly, the client wishes to add a garage that is directly connected to the house. Given the existing configuration of the entry hall, stairway, and the restrictions of the zoning setbacks, the garage will invariably block the front face of the house and constrain the existing open space in the driveway. Also, the dimensions and scale of the garage will tend to dominate and "vehicularize" the whole entry sequence. The clients therefore asked for a garage that could accommodate a different program, should they revert to using the existing carport—hence the idea of the greenhouse or sun-room. It sits in front of the house, on a paved new ground that defines the boundaries of the entry court. Its orientation and crystalline form sustain the primacy of the oblique in a prow-like corner aligned with the driveway. A continuous undulating glass skin covers the garage/greenhouse and travels up the front elevation, bringing light to the main entry space while framing the view of the garage roof from the second floor.

The client, who will serve as the contractor, is intent on controlling the budget by building with economical materials and methods of assembly, in the fashion of a "barn." Office dA's proposal accordingly combines a wood-frame construction system with corrugated galvanized steel. Since the client will be able to offset some of the labor and craft costs, carefully studied and executed details offset the use of common materials. This project thus engages the technology of corrugation as a vehicle of architectural investigation and invention; the aim is to radicalize the spatial, perceptual, and formal possibilities of corrugation in order to overcome its raw and industrial qualities. Hence the various alterations to the material and its conventional usage: they seek to invert the "noble" and the "domestic" in

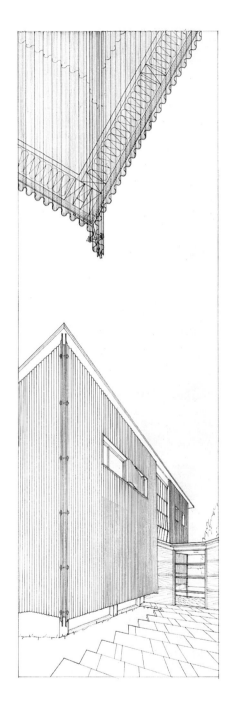
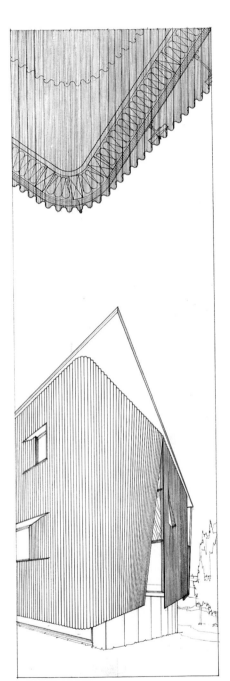
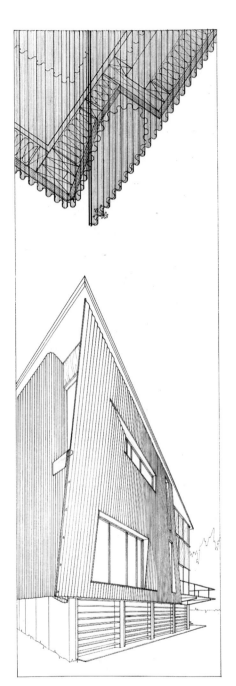

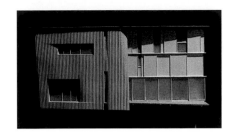

what is customarily utilitarian. The qualities and exigencies of the material are played out in different geometric and spatial problems and most evidently in different cladding conditions at the corners. The corrugation is conceived as a taut skin, holding a very tight and constrained program within. The distortions of the skin reflect programmatic pressures or lighting and ventilating needs. The dining room, for instance, is veiled by perforated corrugation, producing a more formal and anonymous façade while maintaining a clear and uninhibited vista from the inside. The stair access to the yard impacts the skin of the building to produce a covered landing area, mediating between the living room and the outdoors. The corrugation draws back at the southeast corner of the house to expose a balcony overlooking the landscape. So while the corrugated metal is wrapped around the existing house as a thin drape, it is also called on to re-formulate the idea, perception, and space of the house.

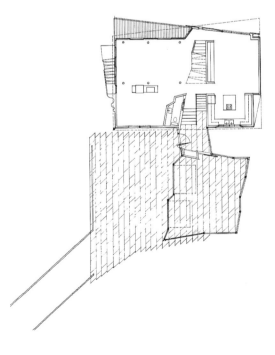

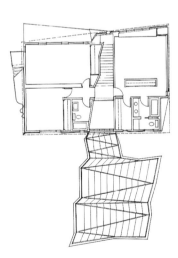

(Opposite Page) Perspectives and detail plan projections of Cufflink corner NE, Bodywrap corner NW, Squeezed corner SW (This Page) First and second floor plan.

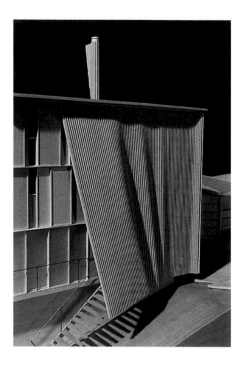
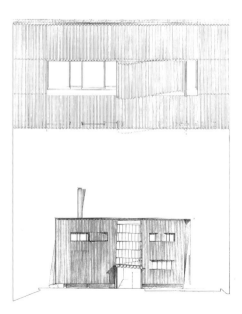
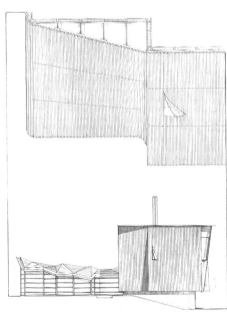
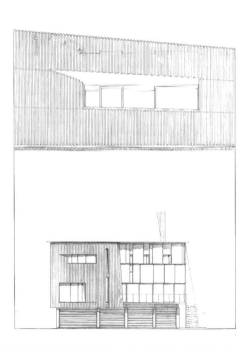

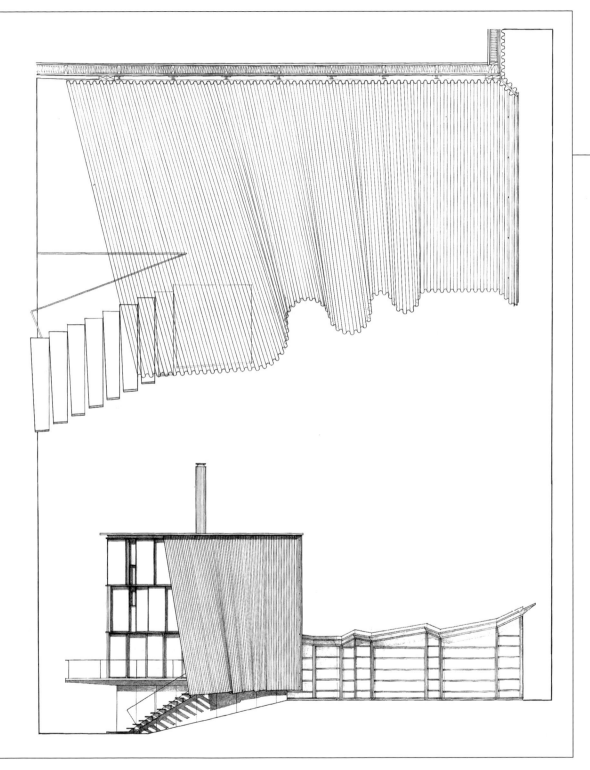

(Opposite) North, West, and South elevation. (This Page) East elevation with corrugated curtain wall detail.

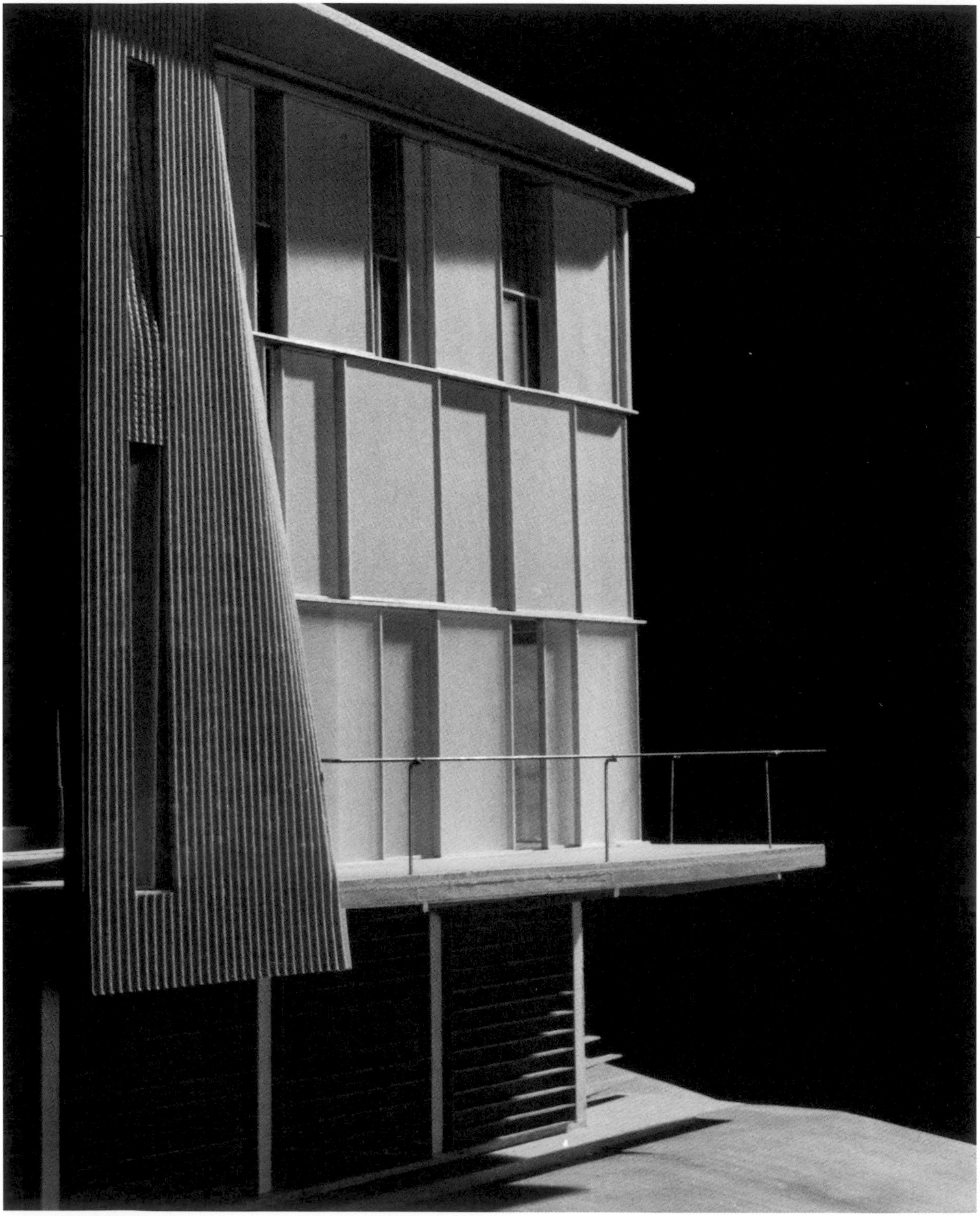

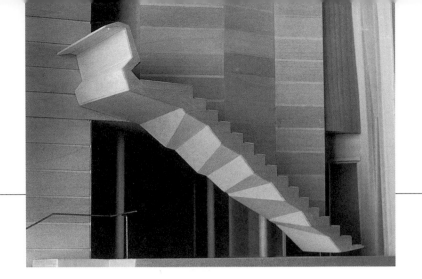

(Opposite Page) Detail of balcony
on south elevation. (This Page Top)
Detail of suspended staircase.
(Middle) View of model section.
(Bottom) Detail view of garage roof
connection to glass curtain wall.

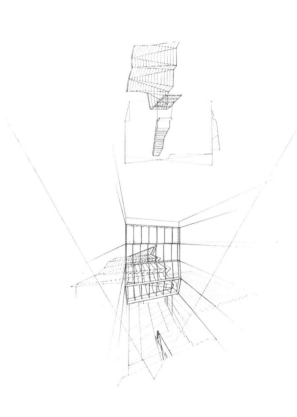

(This Page Top) View of east elevation.
(Middle) Detail of garage. (Bottom)
Sectional view of model.

The Suchart House

This design aims to set up a dialogical relationship with both the landscape and the city by deploying various compositional strategies: framing, unveiling, mimicking, camouflaging, bracketing, and editing. The outcome is a building presenting different attitudes and modes of engagement with the site. The tone ranges from silent reserve to exuberant idiosyncrasy. Since the site is on an extreme slope, the inevitable problem of "cut and fill" evolved as the main source of architectural preoccupation: at a technical level, how to balance the displacement of earth from one portion of the site to another, and at a representational level, how to "architecturalize" the act of cutting into the earth as the paradigmatic image of the house. Thus, a wedge-like space—a virtual cone of vision—is cut into the landscape producing distinct perspectival relationships with both the mountain and the valley: foreshortening and intensifying the view toward the cut into the mountain and splaying out the vista toward the horizon, accentuating the horizontality of the valley. The main spaces of the house occupy this wedge, starting with a courtyard in the hillside, a reflecting pool, the main living area, and an exaggerated balcony that helps to "edit" the immediate foreground from the living room.

Two walls define the edges of the wedge and retain the earth, while a portion of the mountain spills into the courtyard, down along a trough, and into the reflecting pool. The floor of the wedge is made of the stone of the mountain, maintaining a rough and thicker cut in the courtyard, a honed finish in the living room, and a thin polished veneer in the balcony that "drapes" over the edge of the concrete lip cantilever. Thus, the floor embodies the transformation of the mountain from its rough state to its most manipulated condition from the beginning to the end of the wedge. The wedge is partitioned into a series of discreet but continuous spaces separated by a series of veils, screens, and glass walls. A copper mesh curtain unveils the view toward the mountain, while rotating and movable canvas panels articulate the front elevation, rendering the front façade as a mute surface at times and an animated filter at others.

The program of the house is distributed along two "bars" flanking the east and western edge of the wedge, terraced on various split-levels corresponding to the topography of the landscape. All the bedroom areas occupy the western bar, while the family room/kitchen and library occupy the eastern bar, above the garage. Given the terraced organization, each room affords different views of defined landscape features. For instance, the breakfast room overlooks the "canyon," the bedroom bay window frames the "rock," and the library studies the "peak." These special rooms, in turn, function as special attributes for the house, acquiring an iconographic presence and an expressive dimension in excess of the tectonic framework of the house. Most importantly, they partake in the visual strategies of the house by exaggerating and underlining certain features of the context while distilling and editing others.

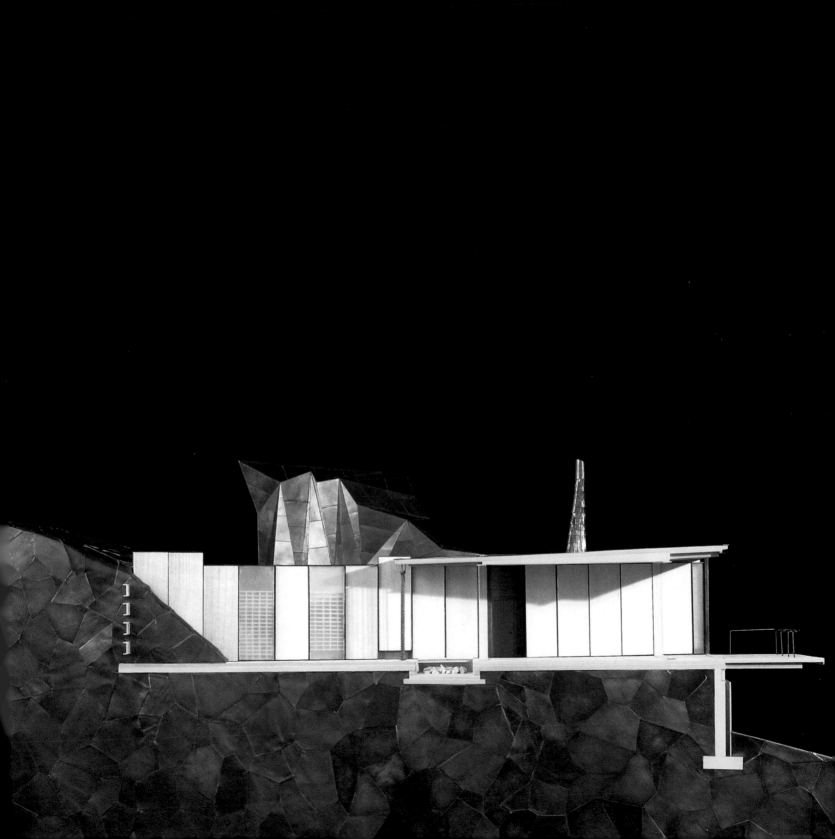

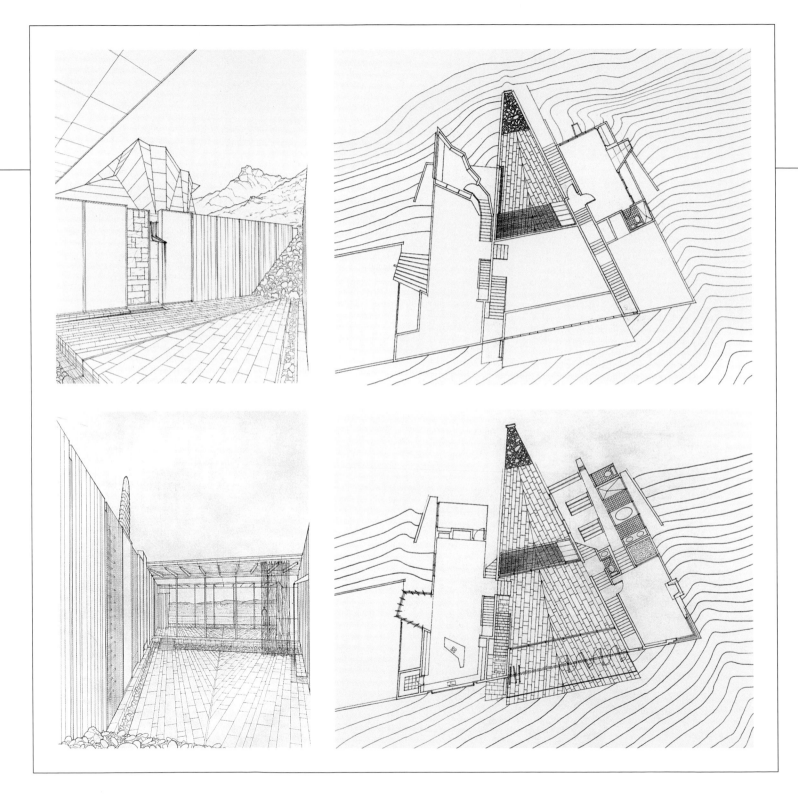

The constructional and tectonic system of the house operates in two distinct rhetorical manners, both of which partake in the visual and perspectival strategies of the house, acquiring a performative function in engaging with the context. The general framework of the house is based on a grid of stone, concrete, and stucco panels that slide, rotate, hinge, pivot, and extrude—all as a way of articulating, framing, or blocking distinct views. Windows and doors have no place in the language of this house; all apertures are a result of some virtual and some literal movement or deviation of the grid of panels. Copper, a natural resource of Arizona, acquires an emblematic status for the house, becoming the frame for each of the panels. At the same time, the use of copper is radicalized in the design of the attributes, as they rupture and break from the formal logic of the panel system. The copper "scales" on the chimney, "twists" on the bay window, "facets" on the library—all allusively evoke the local fauna and, the materiality of the landscape. Among the attributes, the library plays the most prominent role, at once an extension of the copper roof and also an architectural still life, a misplaced rock atop the house. The library thus emerges as a footnote to the view beyond, playing on the ambiguities of camouflage and self-assertiveness, never fully part of the house nor part of the landscape, but an estranged offspring of both.

The design combines two architectural traditions, which have traditionally competed for exclusive legitimacy: The rationalist ideal of an abstracted type here accommodates for the mimetic impulse of a symbolic architecture. By allowing the figure to infiltrate and occasionally subvert the frame, the hybrid architecture of the Suchart House could thus dialogue with the landscape without being confrontational or conciliatory.

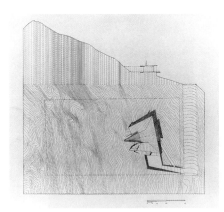

(Opposite Top Left) View of courtyard toward library. (Bottom left) View through courtyard and living area toward the city. (Top right) Second floor plan. (Bottom right) First floor plan. (This Page Top) Front façade movable panels. (Bottom) Site plan and section.

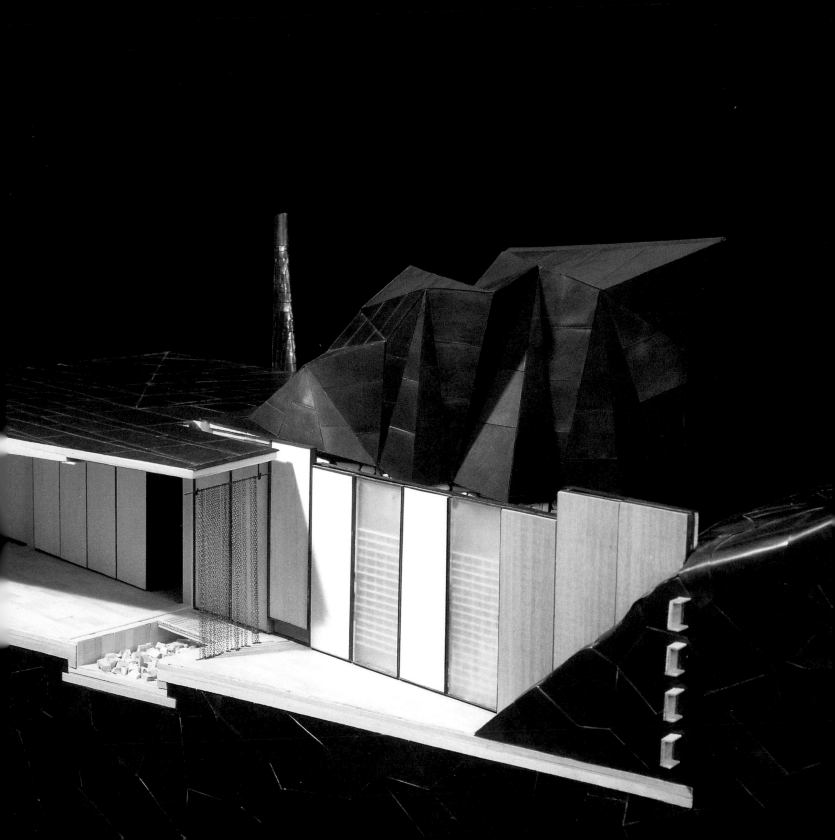

(This Page) View of canyon from library.
(Following Page Top) North-South
section through bedroom suites.
(Bottom) North-South section through
library and kitchen. (Following Spread
Top) Section through courtyard.
(Bottom) North elevation.

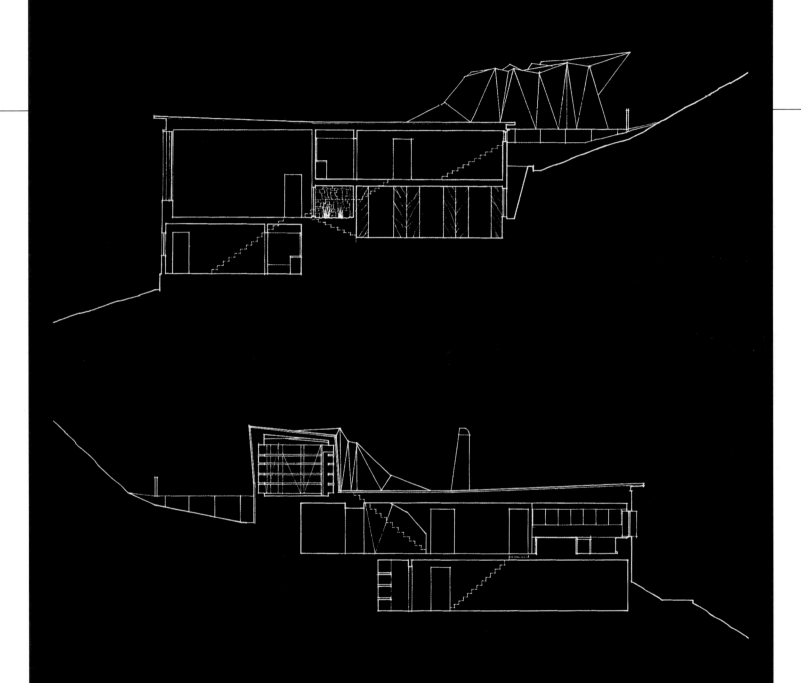

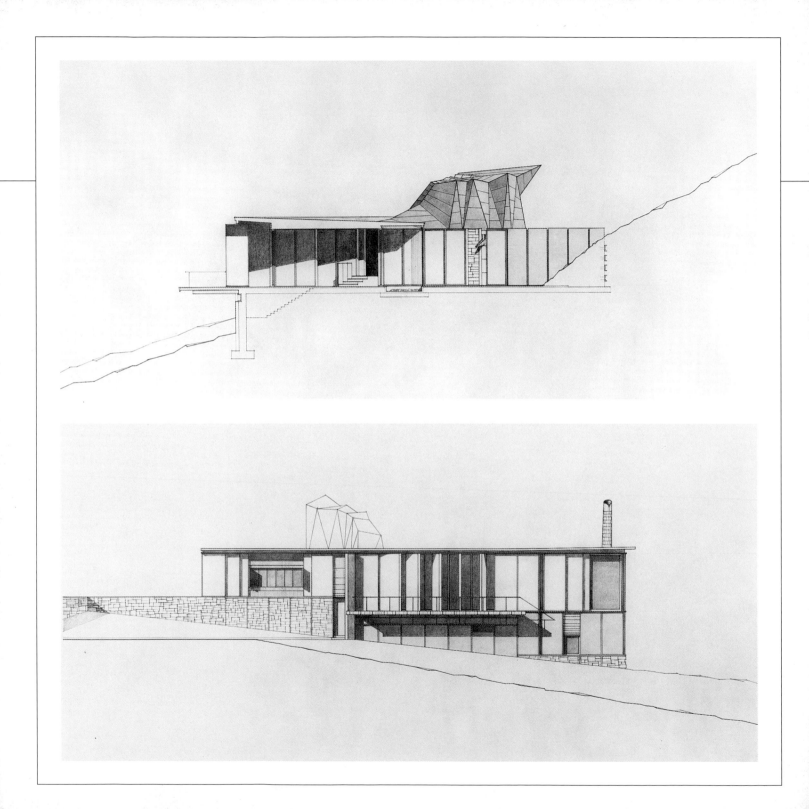

Casa la Roca

Casa la Roca was commissioned by a young family for a suburban lot in Venezuela. It owes its name to the project's main protagonist: a colossal rock that looms over the rear of the property. The rock sits atop of one of the many hills that define the southern edge of Caracas, and its peak affords a spectacular view of the city.

Given the excessive exposure of the site to public views and the limitation in space due to the rock, the aim of the design is to intimate a sense of openness while maintaining adequate privacy and closure for a domestic space. To that end, Office dA took the opportunity to work with terra-cotta block, brick, and tile, pushing their material, tectonic and visual qualities to achieve this twofold objective. The house is wrapped in a continuous surface of terra cotta, except for a large opening carved across from the rock to form an outdoor room of monumental dimensions. This room functions at once as a living space and back yard; shielded from public view and the elements, its faces are clad in continuous bands of sliding glass doors and windows, making its relationship with the building's interior as seamless as possible. The glass membrane is layered with a two-story-high metal sliding security grill system: "steel curtains" that can be drawn to maintain the openness of the house. Tall concrete "bamboo-like" columns support a steel I-beam coffering that suspends the roof aloft.

Thematically, the elevations were designed around three terra-cotta surfaces: the front elevation, the side elevation, and the roof plane. On the southern face, the front elevation is built of terra-cotta blocks that shield the house from the rays of the sun, while eliminating the need for security bars and grills. In addition, the spacing of the blocks is calibrated so that each block may be incrementally rotated to yield special views from any desired location, as evident in the living room; the separated blocks can also be slid to one side to produce the more conventional "punched" opening, as is visible on the second floor. These "billboard-like" effects are actually in a fixed position and only allusively attempt to evoke the occupation of the client. While the front elevation is opened in various moments, its rhetorical intent suggests a mute screen, a textured skin that veils the house's most public face. The side facade is composed of terra-cotta bricks masking the house from the east. The brickwork is laid out in a running bond fashion in the solid area of the living room, and incrementally begins to separate into a voided Flemish bond as it approaches the patio. The geometry of the wall is meant to construct the transition from a load-bearing wall condition to a "serpentine" wall whose undulations produce a structural rigidity while screening the patio elevation. The brick patio wall is drawn back in a "curtain-like" manner suggestive of a theatrical unveiling of the view toward the rock and an openness toward the neighboring plot. Though an uncharacteristic feature in a Venezuelan house, the chimney terminates the brick wall at the front façade and elaborates the undulation of the folded wall; this fireplace, being more of a caprice of the client, is placed more

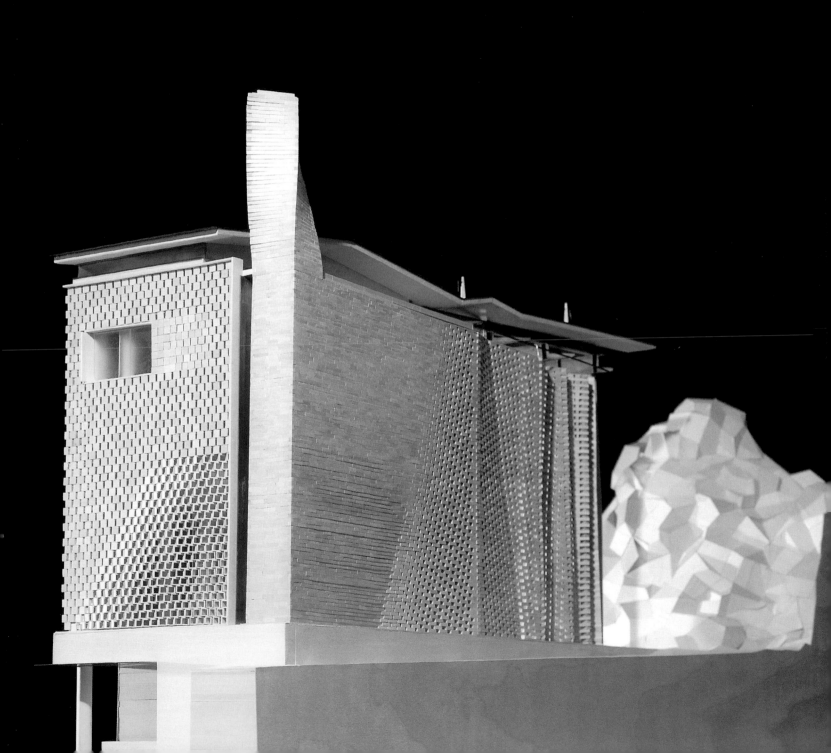

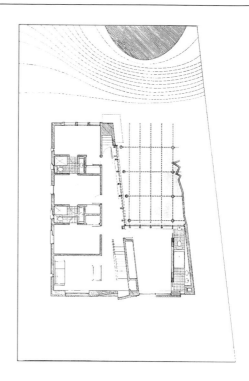

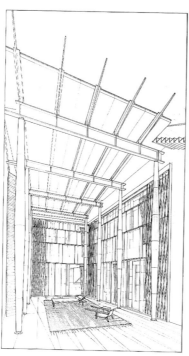

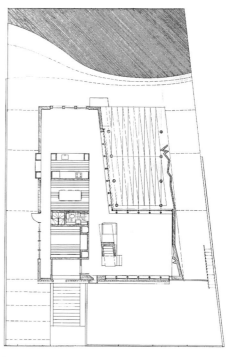

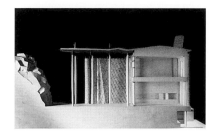

appropriately off-center with the living room and serves efficiently to anchor the corner of the building. The roof is designed with flat terra-cotta tiles and functions much like a "horizontal façade" given the public's vantage point from the rock. Thus each roof pitch corresponds to and shapes a space beneath, producing an undulating "carpet-like" landscape. The flat part of the roof serves as a terrace, and its tiles are detailed in a butt-jointed fashion to maintain a flush profile; as the roof pitches emerge, so too the tiles begin to overlap to drain the water correctly. The roof's border is clad in a copper frame to further objectify the undulating surface. The image of the roof, while suggestive of multiple readings, seeks to preserve a persistent image in "the city of the red tile roofs."

Casa la Roca may be considered a site-specific project with a particular interpretation of its context; in that way, it seeks to bracket, enhance, and capitalize on the natural resources of its surroundings. At the same time, the design foregrounds the necessity of transformation and architectural invention toward the redefinition of that cultural context; thus, while the project argues for a rootedness in local procedures and methods, it insists simultaneously on their redefinition as a way of advancing and extending our knowledge of that place. By working within certain local traditions, materials, and forms, the house is able to communicate its "domesticity"—a quality often lost in "architectural" researches—while demonstrating its "difference" by transcending its functional and programmatic requirements through the "tectonic radicalization" of its material components.

(Opposite Page Top Left) View of terrace from public park. (Top Right) Second floor plan. (Bottom Left) View of outdoor court. (Bottom Right) First floor plan. (This Page Left) Site plan.

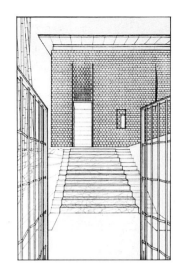

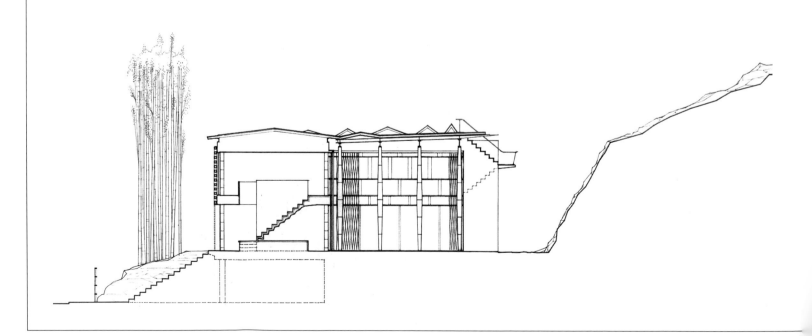

(Opposite) Site section with perspective sequence from main entry up to roof terrace. (This Page) Perspective view of the rock from shaded court.

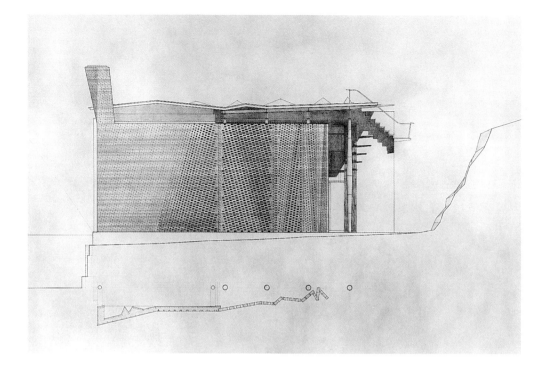

(Top) East elevation. (Bottom) South
elevation. (Opposite Page) Detail view
of terra cotta curtain wall.

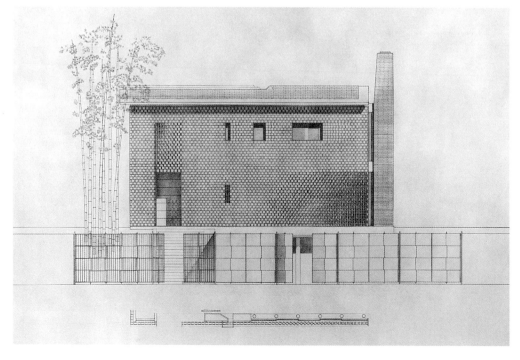

The Mill Road House

This project was commissioned by a developer. It deals with the constructional and financial exigencies of the speculative house. Instead of providing for the standard repertoire of accessories, Office dA invested in design to invent the "features" that would make the house desirable. Standard developer-funded projects customarily rely on dubious amenities such as hot tubs, kitchen appliances, and bathroom fixtures as marketing tools; they promote clichés such as "cathedral ceilings" or "colonial style" decorations as architectural crutches. The house on Mill Road optimizes basic real-estate assets. With minimal means, it transforms various typological and constructional conventions to achieve unprecedented aesthetic and tectonic effects.

Located at the edge of Madison's historic district, the site presents a variety of distinguishing features in what could otherwise be described as a typical suburban environment. The house sits in the last lot on the block, adjacent to the fields of a district school; it hence maintains the conventional frontal relationship with the street while responding to the oblique views toward the west. The program of the house is modest and does not exceed 1,600 square feet (150 square meters), as requested by the client. The first floor consists of an open, flexible plan that accommodates a large living area and a sizable kitchen with a dining area—the dining may alternatively (and comfortably) be part of the living area. Given the inability to afford high ceilings or vertical spaces, the first floor is surrounded by a continuous glass wall to create a horizontal and spatial connection to the landscape. For the sake of privacy, and in response to the Alabama climate, the glass box is guarded by a second layer of cladding: fixed wooden louvers on the north and wood folding doors to the south. Capitalizing on the best location and views at the southwest corner of the house, an exceptionally tall screen porch provides an open-air room characteristic of southern living. The screen of the porch weaves through the structure of the room, giving tectonic definition to the architectural elements and figurative clarity to the use of wood and screen. A stair core acts as the focal point of the interior, substituting for the traditional hearth of Northern climates and expensive masonry construction. The stair is capped by a light shaft, providing an alternative source of light into the living area. While the plan of this house is specific to its site and context, its main footprint (16 by 48 feet/5 by 16 meters) is highly flexible as a prototype and could be built with or without various appendages, as needed.

A certain economy in construction was crucial in conceptualizing the house—minimizing circulation space, foundation work, and masonry work, while pushing the limits of wood-frame construction. In addition, the language and iconography of the house was to be characteristically vernacular, in sympathy with the district's historic preservation society guidelines. The bar-building enabled them to clearly divide the public from the private side of the

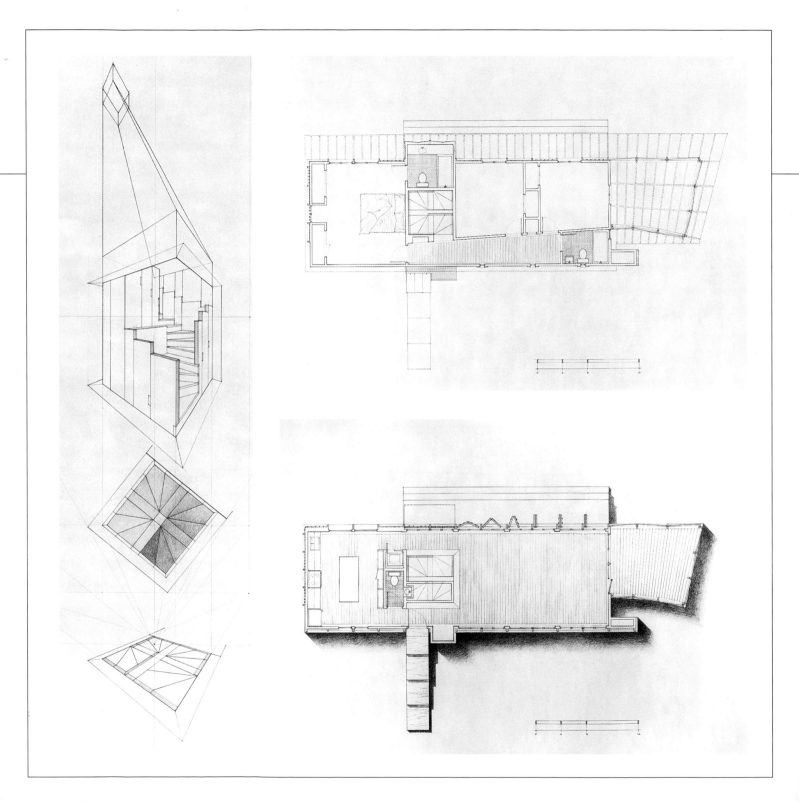

house, defining different strategies for their cladding. The front facade attempts to give a public scale to the street elevation of a house of modest dimensions. Using horizontal wood siding (different sizes of clapboard and clapboard louvered screen) the house filters the image of a "glass house" through its reveals. This apparatus hints at the house's interior while maintaining a formal and shielded face. The south wall, on the other hand, is a transformation of vertically laid wood siding: Tongue and groove panels alternate with board and batten panels, visually extending the weaving pattern of the screen porch. Folding doors (protecting the living areas) and a hinged screen wall shielding the bathroom, articulate the same folding and weaving motif at a smaller scale and contribute to the more informal character of the back. The cladding inventions in the Mill Road House are strategic: since the budget does not allow for generous space, the design explores the architecture of surface; it capitalizes on the tectonics of cladding to project the distinct character and identity of the Mill Road House in the depth of the surface.

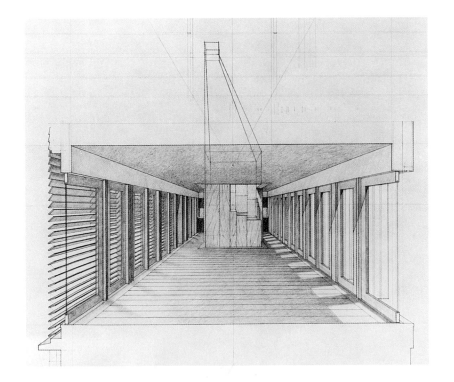

(Opposite Page) Perspective diagram of staircase; second-floor and first-floor plans. (This Page Top) View of front elevation mockup. (Bottom) Sectional perspective of living area toward main stair.

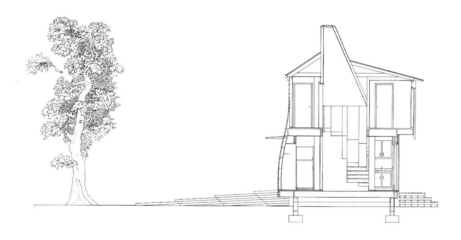

(This Page Top) Detail view of south elevation. (Middle) Section through staircase skylight. (Bottom) West elevation. (Opposite Page) Perspective view and exploded axonometric of screen porch with woven screen through structural members. (Following Spread Top) Front elevation. (Bottom) Back elevation.

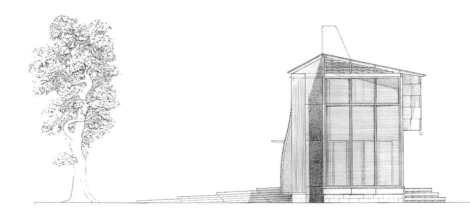

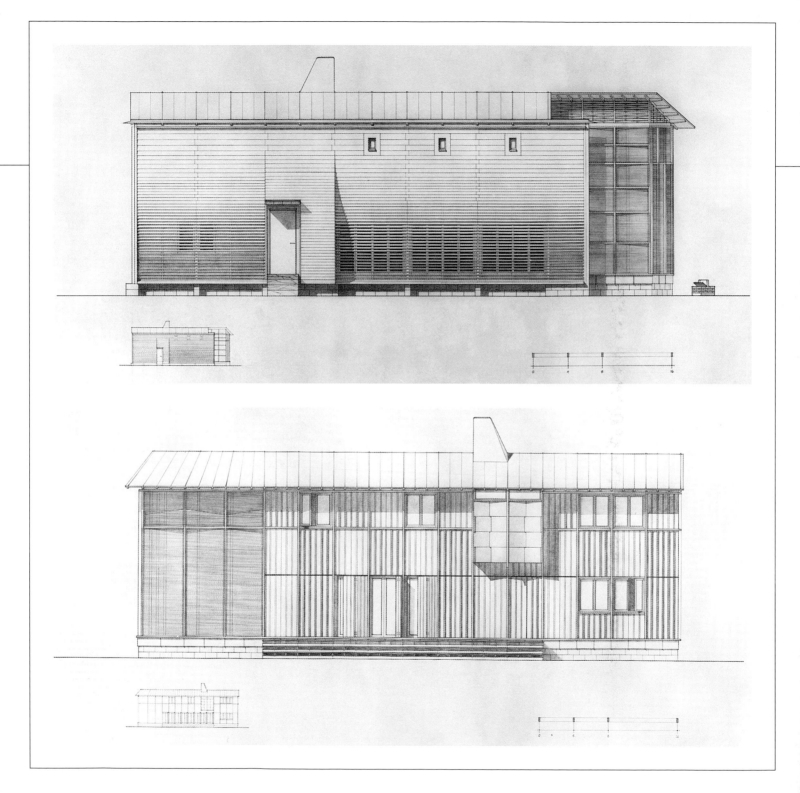

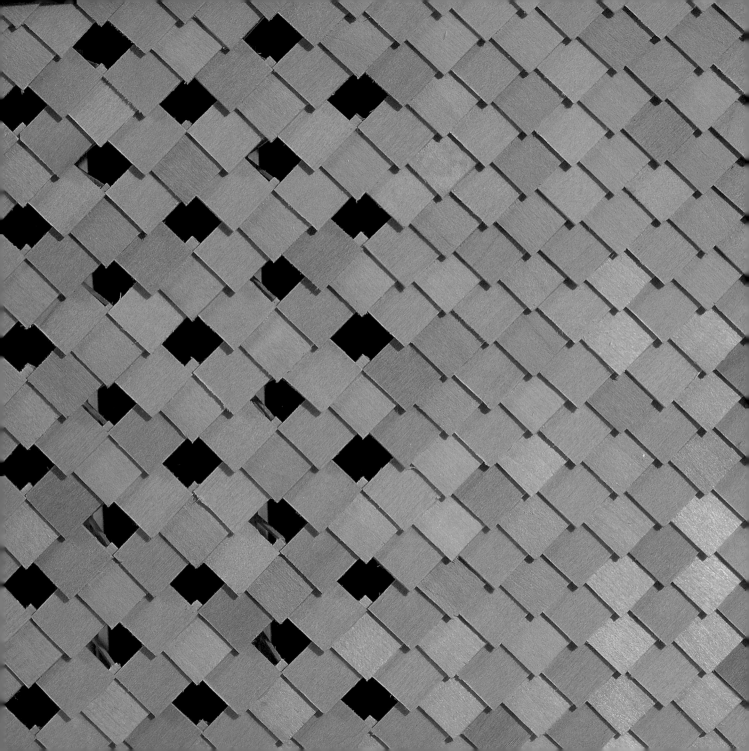

Urban Design ▶

Master Plan for the Town of Wayland

Suburban developments define the majority of inhabited American landscapes, and yet there are very few alternative planning options available beside the recent "new urbanist" strategies, theme-park urbanism, and the prevailing big mall development schemes. This project focuses on suburban typologies, landscapes, and environments as a vehicle for producing an alternative suburbanism. Acknowledging shifts in scale, the unusual adjacencies of building types, and the uniqueness of available open spaces, this project seeks to define a new civic realm in the infrastructure of suburbia. With the end of the Cold War and the downsizing of the military budget, many businesses linked to the defense industry are cutting back and diversifying their investments. Raytheon, the company that developed the famed Patriot missile, has closed its plant in Wayland after forty years in the small New England town. The company has played a central role in supporting the small town, offering a strong tax base, as well as yearly grants to various community activities, including funding for this project.

The Raytheon site was initially developed in the 1950s, a huge corporate "shed" with an even larger parking lot characteristic of many contemporary malls, office parks, and suburban environments. The Raytheon building is a very large structure, built for a single use and with little or no significant urbanistic relationship with the center of Wayland. The site sits northeast of the intersection of Route 127 and Route 20, presently the town center. Given the densification of the suburbs and impact of regional commuter traffic, the quaint "old village" quality of the town has essentially been lost. Route 20 serves as "the strip," a high-speed thoroughfare housing many of the local stores, some franchises, and public services. Route 127, on the other hand, has maintained a rural character because it runs along a corridor protected by the historical preservation district as well as the National Wildlife Refuge. After the closing of the Raytheon plant, the town of Wayland has set up the "Raytheon Committee" to oversee the planning, phasing, and reconfiguration of the Raytheon site over the coming decades with the idea that the site may emerge as a new town center. To that end, a series of focus-group meetings were conducted with a variety of interest groups to research the programmatic, social, and physical needs of the community.

The aspiration of the community is to develop a new town center with distinguished public spaces for ceremonial events as much as for everyday use. The Office dA proposal relies on the features of the landscape, both natural and artificial, suburban and rural, to define and characterize a sequence of public spaces linking Routes 20 and 127.

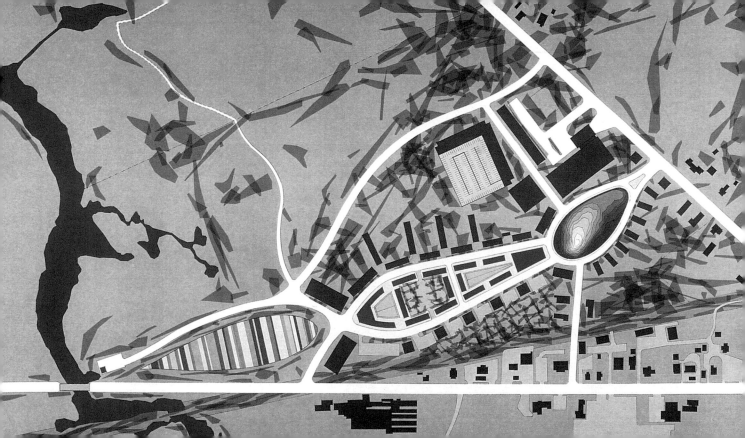

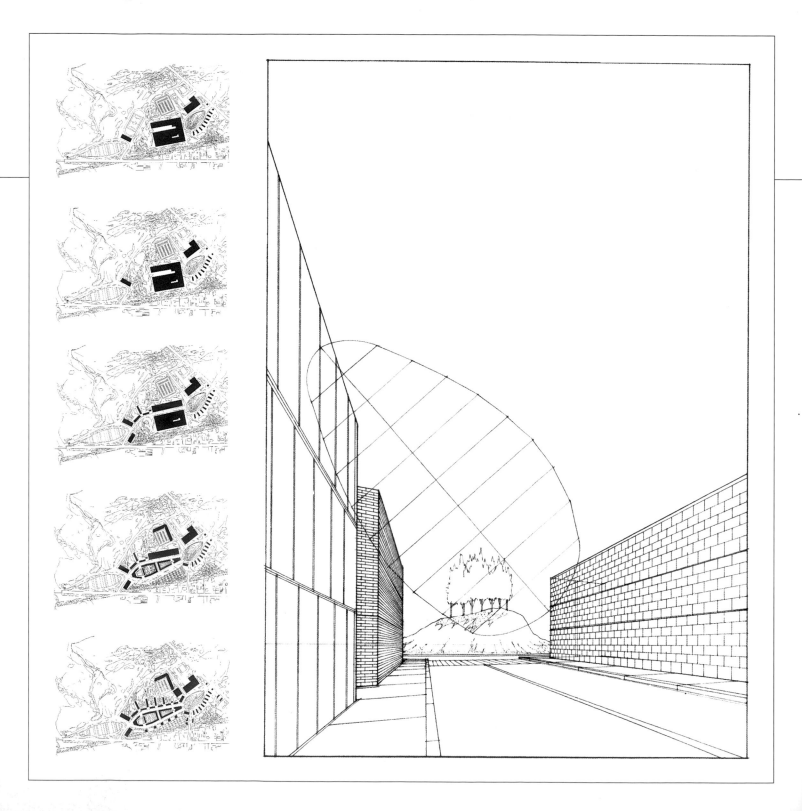

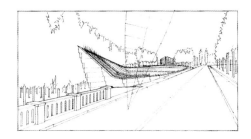

The first, perhaps the most enigmatic is a "knoll" on the eastern edge of the site, a "mass" of earth emerging from the land on Route 127—the remains of a large hill that was cut and flattened when the Raytheon Building was constructed. The "Wayland Knoll" is a focal point and the representative center of the town. The surrounding pavement is designed to frame and de-familiarize this singular geological vestige. On the western edge of the site, the Sudbury River acts as a natural boundary with the Sudbury River Bridge as the gateway into town. The river is presently reached in a quasi-clandestine fashion through an adjacent private property. The town would like to encourage and formalize the access to the river; for ecological reasons, it also aims to regulate and restrict water traffic to a specified category of maritime crafts. The Office dA proposal provides an access road to a public platform on the water, a large dock serving the recreational and functional needs of the waterfront. The new access road is laid along a public green named "Teardrop Meadow." This new ground is a patchwork of various landscape types from the Great Meadows Natural Wildlife Refuge; it serves as a pedestrian access to the water and an emblem of the preservation land. Gradually lifted, tilted, and hence objectified, this "artificial" field contrives a "natural" billboard for the town.

The Teardrop Meadow is "stitched" to the Wayland Knoll by strands of circulation serving the facilities of the new town center. The infrastructure is consistently meant to frame the natural assets of the site. The streets converging at the Knoll and the Meadow mark the fourth corner of the Wayland Crossing. Traffic, in general, is designed to "pause" at each natural episode: the Meadow, the Crossing, the Grove, and the Knoll. Everyday parking is imbedded in a grove of indigenous evergreen trees, planted in the column-grid fashion of a garage. The block of mixed-use buildings may be developed in small parcels, or more probably as a single entity, considering the nature and scale of contemporary projects. Its slim and elongated profile produces an edge with a continuous street frontage, extending the pedestrian sequence from one public space to another. The end-buildings of the block are designated as public, and the majority of housing is oriented toward the landscape along the northern edge. The Public Safety Building is located on the northern edge of the Wayland Knoll with direct access to Route 20. In short, the aim of this project is to invest in the "infrastructure" of the town, both natural and built, as a means of revitalizing its economic, physical, and civic potentials. To that end, the natural assets of the surrounding landscape are recast in their "surreal" potential: the interventions highlight certain qualities that can be extraordinary, given the right frame, but which now lay dormant and under-utilized. The public spaces hence created are hybrid in nature and character. They "float" somewhere between the natural landscape and the sub-urban realm, staking out a new territory for mutant morphologies and unclassifiable but dignified environments.

(Opposite Page) Phasing diagrams and perspective view of Wayland knoll from proposed street. (This Page) View of Teardrop Meadow from Sudbury River bridge.

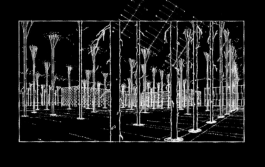

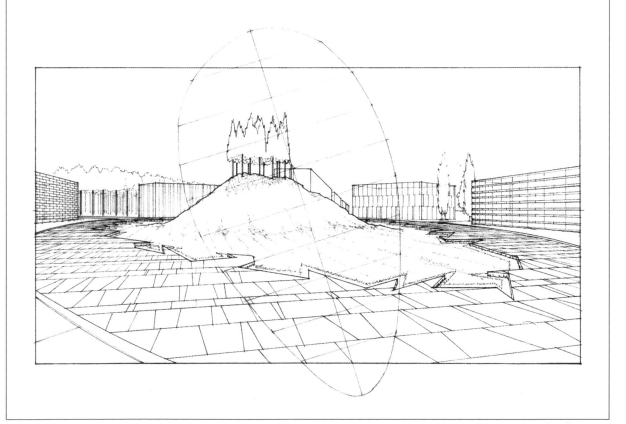

(Opposite Page) Collage of
parking grove. (This Page)
View of Wayland knoll.

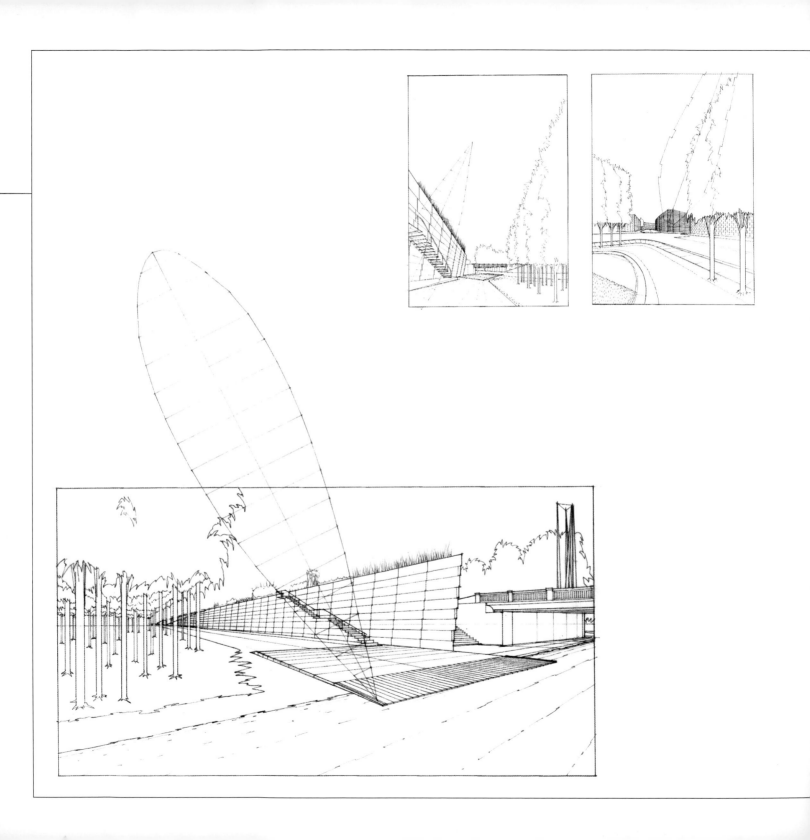

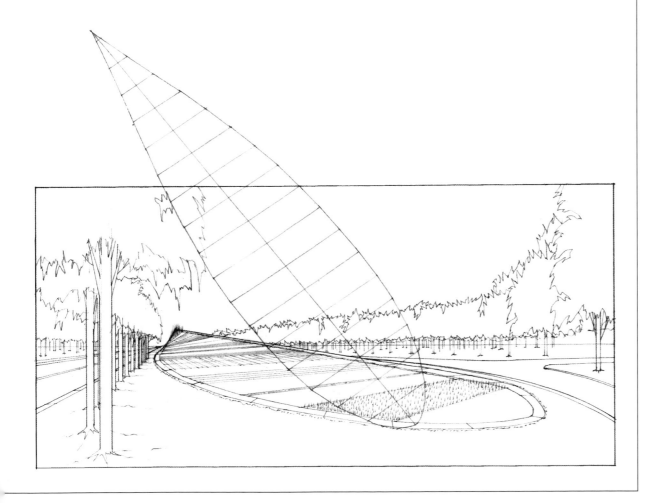

(Opposite Page Top Left) View toward boat launch along Teardrop Meadow retaining wall. (Top Right) View toward proposed urban block from Teardrop Meadow. (Bottom) View of boat launch on Sudbury River. (This Page Left) View of Teardrop Meadow from proposed intersection.

Miami: Public Infrastructure for the Tropics

MIAMI, FLORIDA

The presence of infrastructural elements—highways, commuter rail systems, bus stations, etc.—has long been a fact of the contemporary city. Yet one finds few examples in recent history where these objects' massive presence has been addressed in urbanistic or architectural terms. The realm of infrastructure has all too often been relegated to the domain of the civil and traffic engineer, whose disciplines do not have the means to address more fully the complexities—architectural and social—involved in planning the city.

As a result, while cities' infrastructures have developed a great deal in the past three decades, they have grown with negligence and to the detriment of urbanistic and public aspects of the city. For instance, even though many highways have successfully connected the city's districts at a regional level, they have failed to account for the relationship between neighboring communities through (and over) which they have intervened. Furthermore, since they have been designed for the "automobile" (inevitably resulting in colossal dimensions), they have never been "scaled" to accommodate pedestrians and other inhabitants. This has resulted in the vast expanse of wasted space under, around, and between most major infrastructural interventions in the city.

Office dA's proposal takes three different places in Miami and addresses some of the programmatic, urbanistic, and architectural potentials of infrastructure. This proposal first operates at a planning level, attempting to reintroduce Miami's public—through infrastructure—to one of its great natural resources, the Miami River. Secondly, this proposal deals with the transformation of three typical pieces of infrastructure—the highway overpass for Florida Route 836, the drawbridge (Miami Ave.), and the elevated Metrorail (proposed for the port)—as catalysts for public life; while their alteration is tailored to the particularities of site and climate, these solutions—for which there are no precedents—are meant to address problems prevalent in many contemporary cities. Since each piece of infrastructure was found to have some latent memorable quality, each design proposal draws on that potential to give them a renewed public "identity" through architectural definition. The iconographic specificity of each proposal was seen as rhetorically crucial to create a link with Miami's history, but also to give an air of reality and a sense of cultural relevance to schemes that may otherwise remain utopian.

HIALEAH

MIAMI

MIAMI

KEY BISCAYNE

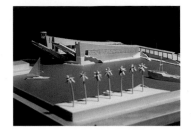

THE MIAMI AVENUE DRAWBRIDGE

The Miami Avenue Drawbridge is a remarkable piece of infrastructure: a six-lane drawbridge that opens in four different segments. Their action is particularly spectacular because of the diagonal relationship to the river and their consequent misalignment in the tilted position.

Notwithstanding the technological display, the Miami Avenue Drawbridge is ill-equipped to connect Miami's two financial districts, Brickell and downtown Miami, in a significant urban fashion. The plan recasts the drawbridge as a full-fledged public amenity that would perform beyond the mere provision for vehicular traffic and improve the relationship between the city and the Miami River.

The drawbridge is altered by the introduction of flanking arcades that house fisheries, bus stops, and seating areas for the viewing of the Miami River. The arcades bring to the water the kind of urban life characteristic of Miami's neighborhoods. The plan also proposes a public marina around the bridge with the intent of exploiting the much neglected—and privatized—river for public use. This public space is defined by a continuous canopy that would allow cars and pedestrians to freely move along the water's edge.

(This Page Top) View of Miami Avenue Marina. (Bottom) Miami Avenue Drawbridge site plan. (Opposite Page) View of Miami Avenue Bridge, arcade, and promenade toward public outlook.

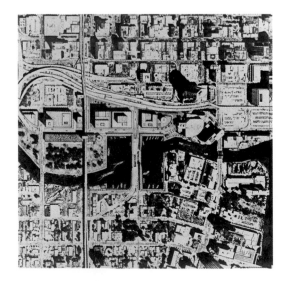

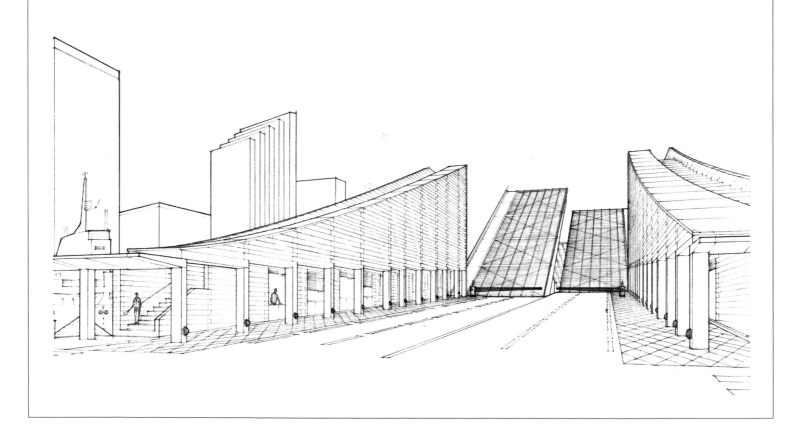

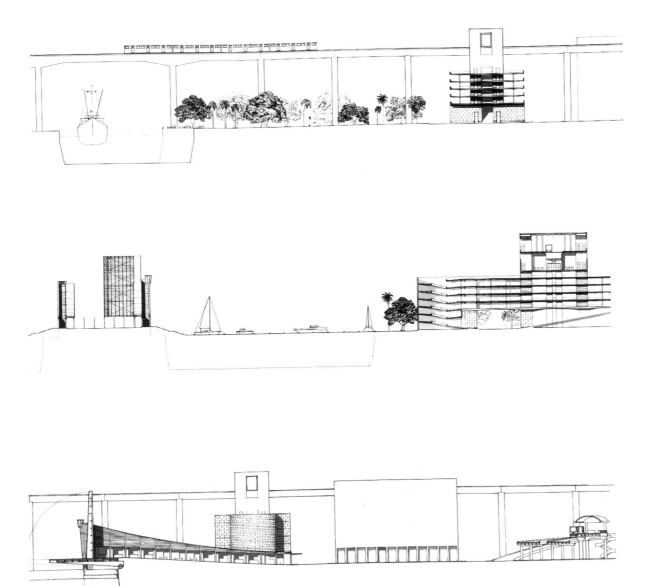

(Opposite Page Top Left) View of Miami Avenue bridge from marina. (Top Middle) View of waterfront park through portal of commuter station. (Top Right) View of marina from public outlook. (Bottom) View of Miami Avenue drawbridge from downtown intersection. (This Page Top) North-south section through commuter station. (Middle) East-west section through Miami Avenue arcade and commuter station. (Bottom) North-south section through Miami Avenue.

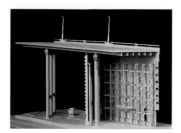

THE 836 OVERPASS

The 836 Overpass is a unique feature of one of Miami's most traveled highways. As it crosses the Miami River, the highway dramatically rises to great heights to allow for the masts of sailboats to pass below. The space created underneath the highway is of monumental dimensions; it could be described as a hypostyle hall had it not been so utilitarian in character.

The highway overpass is also adjacent to two significant public institutions: the Orange Bowl and the Dade County Courthouse. A redesigned 836 Overpass uses the existing highway as a means of connecting these public buildings to the Miami River.

On the north bank of the river, the unusual height of the highway provides an opportunity for creating a public hall. This screened space, which accommodates activities associated with the river, such as a market and boat storage, serves to define a public square across the courthouse. On the south bank of the river, the underbelly of the highway is programmed with a parking garage and recreational facilities. They serve the proposed athletic complex and the adjacent stadium.

(This Page Top) View of boat storage scaffolding. (Bottom) 836 Overpass site plan. (Opposite Page) View of model showing corner connection between shingled concrete curtain wall and load-bearing precast concrete wall.

(This Page Top) Riverfront view.(Middle Left): Detail of riverfront elevation with precast concrete units. (Middle Right): View of Market Hall underneath highway.(Bottom) Courthouse plaza elevation. (Opposite Page Top) Perspective views of the 836 overpass. (Bottom) North-south section through Courthouse Plaza, Market Hall, and bus stop; East-west section through highway, boat storage, and Market hall and; North-south section through highway parking garage and Orange Bowl.

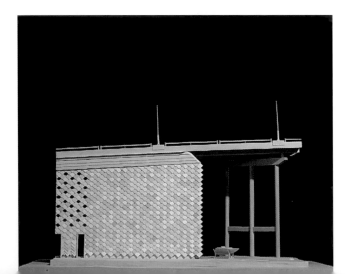

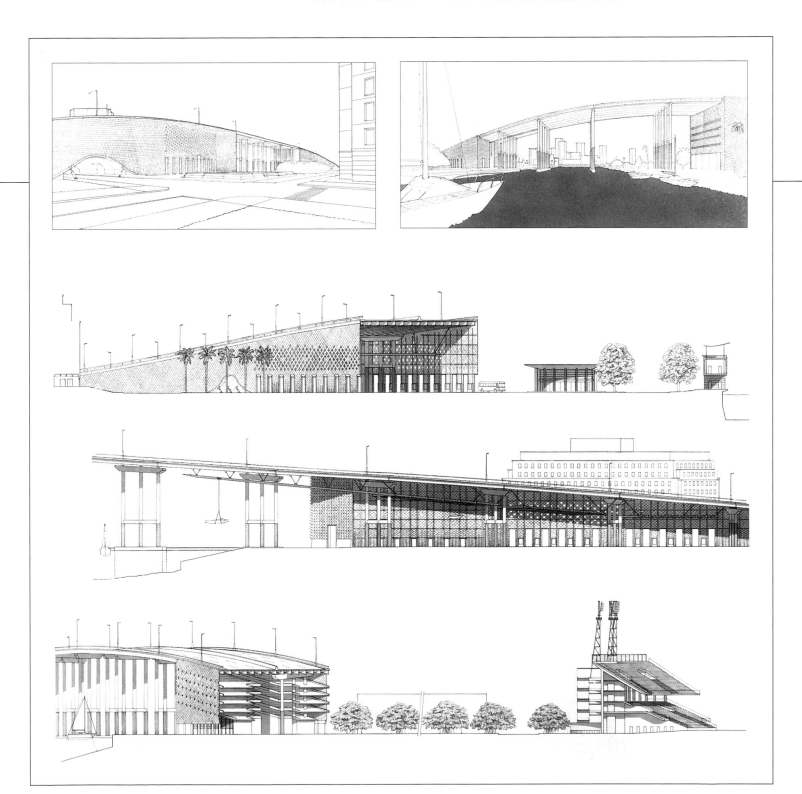

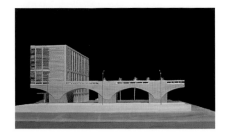

THE METRORAIL ARCADE

Unlike in other cities, Miami's light-rail system could not be developed underground because of unfavorable soil conditions. Instead, the Metrorail is elevated above the ground, sometimes to remarkable heights and with considerable benefits: the panoramic overview offered to riders is a valued asset indeed, considering the predominance of the horizontal in the city's public realm.

This case study proposes a new Metro-mover system for the Port of Miami, which to date is not accessible by public transit. The proposal promotes significant relationships between the Metro-mover and the adjacent amenities: the port terminals and the main access road. Reorganizing the site along the Metro-mover, the proposal defines the edge of a street on one side, and a green boulevard on the other. The piers of the elevated structure incorporate facilities to activate the boulevard in the manner of an arcade. The relationship between the elevated tracks, station, and parking is carefully considered. Instead of surface parking, each Metrorail station comes with a parking garage. These structures, featuring retail facilities on the ground level, also organize the site by providing visual connections between the cruise ship terminals, the rail stations, and the boulevard.

(This Page Top) Boulevard elevation.
(Bottom) Site Plan of Miami Port.
(Opposite Page) Park elevation.

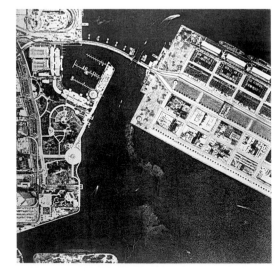

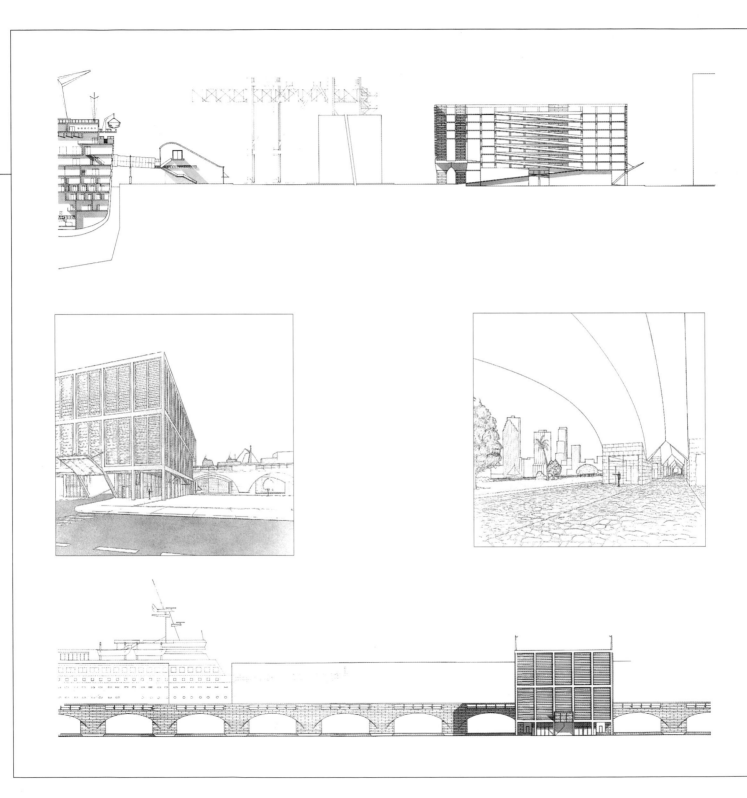

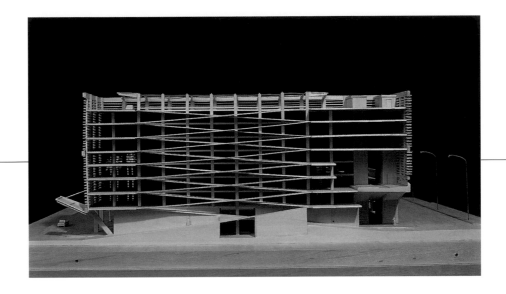

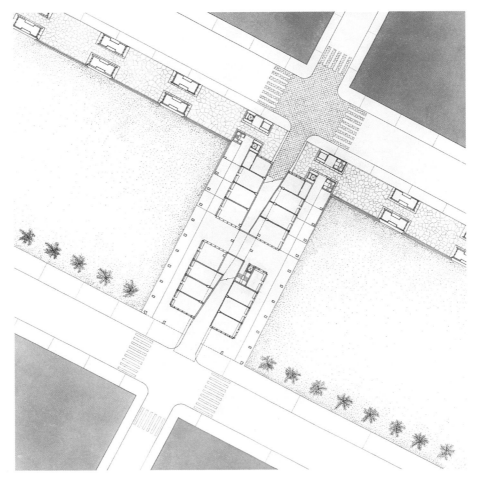

(Opposite Page Top) North/South section from ship terminal to Metrorail station. (Middle Left) View of garage access and pedestrian arcade from boulevard. (Middle Right) View of retail underneath metrorail structure. (Bottom) Elevation of Metrorail arcade and station. (This Page) Site plan.

Roxbury Community Center

BOSTON, MASSACHUSETTS

This project is concerned with urbanity or, more precisely, with its diverse manifestations and means of production. Proceeding with the assumption that urbanity is desirable—despite its conspicuous absence from most new developments—and that although known to occur spontaneously, it can and must be cultivated or catalyzed with artificial means (programmatic, architectonic, and scenographic).[1] This proposal capitalizes on the width of the existing boulevard by inhabiting the median, urbanizing it with programs, building types, and spaces that cater to both the pedestrian and the car. The aim is to "put into architecture"—to architecturalize—the rituals of everyday life (strolling on the sidewalk, playing cards, sitting at a cafe table, playing table tennis, etc.) These activities are cultivated in an open hall of tables—an array of horizontal precast concrete slabs—where density, accessibility, and open-endedness are bound to promote the kind of heterogeneity and spontaneity that fosters urban life. The slabs suggest a variety of possible uses: on level with the sidewalk, they read as an extension of the public ground, an objectification of the lowest common denominator of the public realm. Their height and proportion also accommodates for eating, playing table tennis, and other activities associated with "tables." In effect, the slabs serve as infrastructure for the neighborhood's social activities. The top of the building houses a multi-function hall with two levels around a courtyard, serving the ceremonial and daily needs of the community. The building monumentalizes those quotidian functions in a colossal table—a shelter for the urban life of the infant tables underneath and the community they serve. The courtyard above is shaded by a baldacchino-type canopy.

The building has a composite structure, combining a field of steel mushroom-columns with precast concrete pylons at the corners. The latter house the elevator and stair cores at the corners. The building is surfaced in precast panels of concrete, equal in dimension to the tables at the base of the building. The same panels may thus be seen extending the ground of the sidewalk seamlessly into the stairwells—they are both wall supports and stair landings—wrapping the main hall above, and finally crowning the building with a coping. The geometric pattern on the building's elevation results from the structural and compositional permutations of a single building unit, serving as both vertical and horizontal surface as they negotiate the stairs and landings. In its ubiquity and overstated polyvalence, it is meant to allegorize the "public" realm, but also, and most literally, erect the public ground into a public building. The building is a hybrid type composed of a hypostyle hall, a courtyard, and a baldacchino structure stacked on top of each other in an unlikely but somehow convincing manner. Cohesion is here due to a stubborn insistence on the "table" as an allegorical, typological and figurative theme: table as furniture, table as a monumental shelter, table as a shading canopy—and table as a public platform.

---

1. The thesis of this project was developed from a brief written by Rodolfo Machado for a studio conducted at Harvard University in 1990.

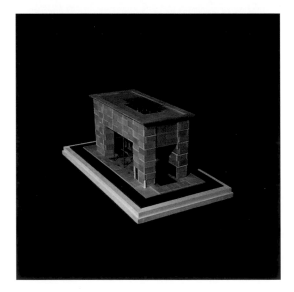

(This Page) Models and exploded axonometric views. (Opposite Top Left) transverse section.(Middle Left) Plan. (Bottom Left) Longitudinal section. (Right) View of Table Hall. (Following Page Top Left) View of community room. (Bottom Left) View of community center.(Right) Axonometric detail of precast panel system with stair landings and windows.

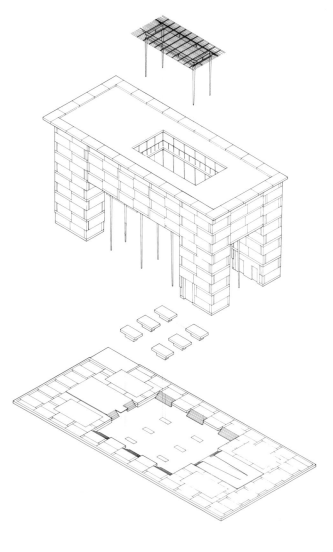

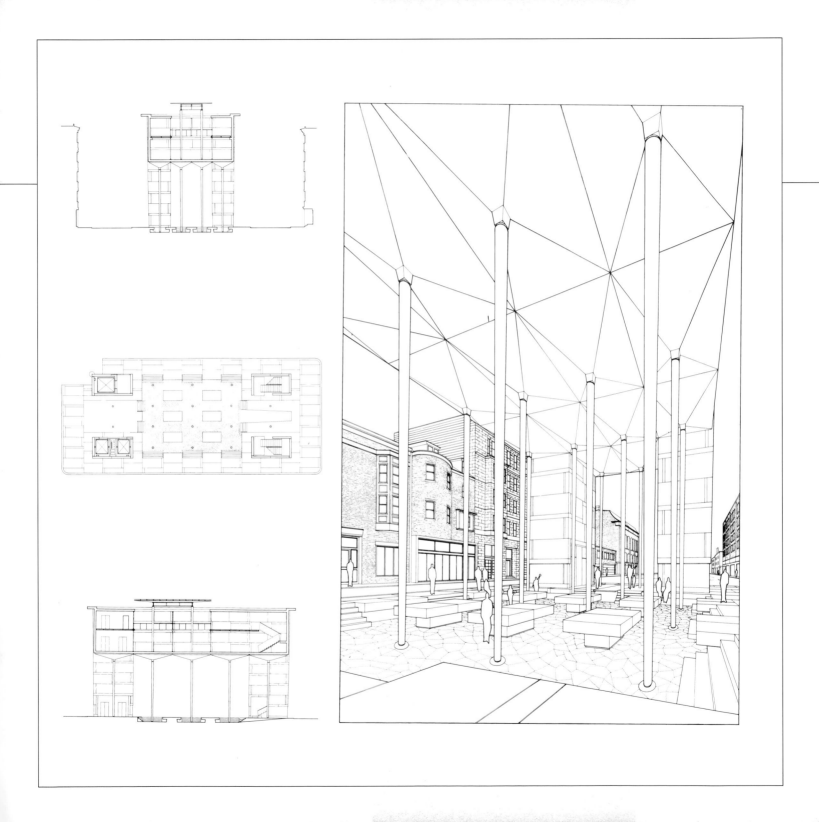

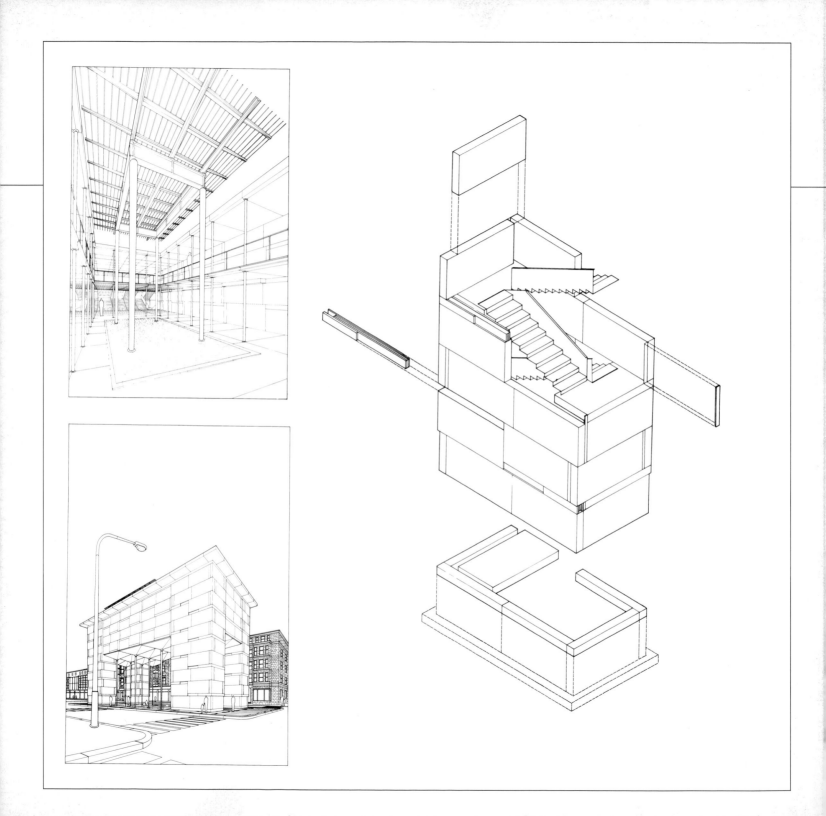

List of Works and Credits

FABRICATIONS: THE TECTONIC GARDEN, "FABRICATING COINCIDENCES"
1996–1998, Museum of Modern Art. New York, New York
Project Design: Mónica Ponce de León, Nader Tehrani
Design Team: Matt LaRue, project coordinator; Tim Dumbleton, animation; Jay Berman, Richard Lee, Jill Porter, Christian Schaller, Phillip Smith, Lee Su
Consultants: Bruce Gitlin, Milgo Bufkin, metalwork; Michael J. Theiss, P.E., The Office of James Ruderman LLP, structural engineer
Fabrication Team: Bruce Gitlin, principal; Alex Kveton, project manager
Computer Layout: Etlana Ostrovski, Wayne Lapierre
Punching: Raphael Franco
Assembly: Tony Pikulinski, Henry Burek, Pawel Burek
Installation: Milgo Bufkin, Office dA, Shahin Barzin, Achille Rossini, Joel Schmidt, Timothy Clark
Photography: Dan Bibb, except page 34 by Michael Moran

INTER-FAITH SPIRITUAL CENTER
1994–1998, Boston, Massachusetts
Awards: 1996 BSA Unbuilt Architecture Award, International Illumination Design Award, 1999; Faith and Form Religious Art and Architecture Design Award, 1999
BSA Young Architects Award, 1999
Client: Northeastern University Spiritual Life Center
Project Design: Mónica Ponce de León, Nader Tehrani
Project Coordinator: Richard Lee
Project Team: Erik Egbertson, Ben Karty, computer drawings; Jill Porter, Jeffrey Asanza, working drawings; Yeong La, model; Patricia Szu-Ping Chen, dome mock-up; Thamarit Suchart, curtain wall mock-up; David Kunzig, Dana Manoliu, Salvatore Rafone, Phillip Smith, Rusty Walker, Timothy Clark
Architect-of-Record: Smart Architecture, Margaret Smart Booz, George Thrush, Nathan Bishop
Architectural Consultant: Brad Johnson
Engineers: Le Messurier Consultants, Peter Cheever, Joe Vercellone
Lighting Consultants: Lam Partners Inc., Paul Zaferiou, Glenn Heinmiller
Mechanical Engineers: Cosentini Associates LLP, Richard P. Leber, Frank Teebagy, P.E.
Acoustical Consultants: Acentech, Douglas H. Sturz
General Contractor: Tom Fitzgerald, Project Superintendent
Woodworking: Michael Perra Inc., Garnet Construction Company Inc.
Glass: Native Sun, Dan & Irene Wheeler
Suspended Domes: M.D.N. Co, Michael Colombo, Office dA, Richard Lee, Phillip Smith
Metalwork, Footwash: Milgo Bufkin, Bruce Gitlin, Alex Kveton
Furniture: Northeastern University Carpentry Shop
Carpets: M. Shirinian
Northeastern University Project Manager: Sally Keeler
Photography: Dan Bibb, Joe Cirillo, Richard Lee, Thamarit Suchart

OSCAR RIERA OJEDA FURNITURE COLLECTION
Client: Oscar Riera Ojeda
Project Design: Mónica Ponce de León, Nader Tehrani
Project Team: Richard Lee, coordinator, Jess Smith, assistant
Fabrication: George Brin, Milgo Bufkin
Photography: Dan Bibb

THE TOLEDO HOUSE
1998–1999, Bilbao, Spain
Award: Progressive Architecture Citation, 1999
Client: Mr. and Mrs. Toledo
Project Design: Mónica Ponce de León, Nader Tehrani
Model Coordinator: Phillip Smith
Project Team: Richard Lee, Jill Porter, Lee Su, Jeffrey Asanza, Kayoko Ohtsuki, Mario D'Artista, Patricia Szu-Ping Chen, Thamarit Suchart, Kristen Giannattasio, Chris Arner, Jennifer Cho, Karen Hock, Jess Smith, Mariko Yoshii, Matt LaRue, Victor Sant'Anna, Jake Cormier, Sergio Rodriguez, Christian Dagg
Photography: Dan Bibb

THE ZAHEDI HOUSE
1997–1998, Weston, Massachusetts
Awards: Progressive Architecture Award, 1998; BSA Young Architects Award, 1999
Client: Kamran and Shirin Zahedi
Project Design: Mónica Ponce de León, Nader Tehrani
Model Coordinators: Jeffrey Asanza, Phillip Smith
Project Team: Richard Lee, Jill Porter, Lee Su
Photography: Dan Bibb, Richard Lee

THE SUCHART HOUSE
1996, Phoenix, Arizona
Client: Dr. and Mrs. Suchart
Project Design: Mónica Ponce de León, Nader Tehrani
Project Coordinators: Thamarit Suchart, Patricia Szu-Ping Chen
Model Team: Jeffrey Asanza, coordinator; Mario D'Artista, Michael Autrey, Joelle Byrer, Kristen Giannattasio, Richard Lee, Kazuyo Oda, Mark Pasnik, Lee Su, Diego Toledo
Associate Architect: Will Bruder, Architect
Photography: Dan Bibb, Richard Lee, Thamarit Suchart

Appendix